Loving Daddy

by

Niki Jordan

1663 LIBERTY DRIVE, SUITE 200
BLOOMINGTON, INDIANA 47403
(800) 839-8640
WWW.AUTHORHOUSE.COM

First published by AuthorHouse 09/17/04

ISBN: 1-4184-9291-4 (sc)

Library of Congress Control Number: 2004111483

Printed in the United States of America
Bloomington, Indiana

This book is printed on acid-free paper.

Acknowledgements

How does one go about personally thanking everyone that has touched their heart in a very significant way?

To my husband: You have lived a lot of this story with me, and so many other stories as well. I thank you for always loving me and sharing this adventure called life with me. I love you.

To my son and my daughter: You are both two of the best gifts that I have ever been given. You bring so much to my life, and I love you. Without your joy, laughter, and your love, life without you would be plain boring.

To all the special angels here on earth, in the form of treasured friends:

Tammy: Your soul is so connected to my own and your heart is pure and loving. It's no wonder I love you.

Jackie: Strong, yet gentle, always giving, never asking for anything in return. You and Matt came into my life when I desperately needed you, and I didn't even know it. You are always in our hearts.

Annette & Chuck: Neighbors first, friends forever.

Paula: We've come a long way, baby. Thanks for all your love.

Becky: Thanks for all you've been and will always be, to me.

Janelle: You are beautiful, inside and out.

B.J.: You allow my free spirit to be just that.....free.

"Jewels": Always the beautiful gem, inside and out, you lift me up.

Galilee: A cut above the rest.

To friends at Redeemer, Trinity, CLC, and Holiday Lakes, God loves you and so do I.

Special thanks to Dean, Bob, and Kendra, and everyone at Authorhouse who helped with this book. You sure made all this much easier ☺

Misty and Lexi: my two four-legged children. You guys are a riot ☺

Foxxy: My beautiful four-legged angel with the sweet smile. I miss you.

Last but not least: To daddy, my special angel. I thank God for you, and for all our happy memories. I miss you and I love you.

Table of Contents

Introduction

This is a true story, and, aside from the names that have been changed, all of the events in this story happened just as they have been explained.

Grief, pain, illness, sadness, and abuse play large parts in this story.

Abuse breaks hearts and destroys relationships. It can break a person's spirit. Thankfully, the human spirit is stronger than any of us know.

Love really DOES conquer all. The greatest gift a parent can give their child is their unconditional love. There is no greater, more liberating gift in this life, than knowing you are loved, just the way you are.

Because in the end, love is all that matters.

Love never ends.

Chapter 1: Preparing for the worst: April 19, 2000

Having left a balmy 80 degrees, I knew it would be chilly in Chicago, but that's all I knew for sure.

As I waited for the plane to take off, my thoughts turned once again to my dad. I couldn't help but wonder what kind of shape I would find him in, once I got back to Indiana and the hospital where he lay, fighting for his life. For the hundredth time, I prayed that I would not be too late. The flight grew bumpy the closer we got to Chicago, and I found the weather to be as dismal as my mood. The captain announced that it was raining and 50 degrees. Lovely, I thought; welcome back.

I hurried off the plane, and finding my sister and sister-in-law waiting for me, we headed out of Chicago.

After dropping my sister-in-law off at her car, we went straight to the hospital. My sister wanted to give me some time with dad, since I had not seen him yet.

My mother was standing in the doorway of my dad's room, and she didn't seem happy to see me at all. Then, with the usual venom in her voice, she asked me what "she" was doing here. Meaning my sister. The thing to understand is that my mom has made a career out of hating everyone in my dad's family. His siblings were no good, and his two biological children from his first marriage, were even worse, as far as she could tell. She, of course, had done nothing wrong, and could never understand why my sister and brother and their families had had nothing at all to do with her and my dad for the past 10 years. To say that this was quite a time for everyone was an understatement.

Unbeknownst to my mom, I had called my brother and sister while I was still in Texas to relay the news about dad, and, to protect me, they told her that they had heard about it through someone else. They were grateful that I had let them know, because my mother had made it very clear for quite some time, that she would never tell them if dad ever got sick, and I totally disagreed with that. I felt that they had every right to know.

Without skipping a beat, my mom started in on me, practically blocking the entrance to dad's hospital room. Frustration was quickly settling in, since all I wanted was to see my dad. She made a point to tell me how selfish I was for taking my trip, and told me that this was all my fault. I was used to being her scapegoat my entire life, so this came as no big surprise.

I moved past my mom finally, and went over to dad's bedside. When I looked at him, shock seemed to reverberate throughout my entire body. He seemed barely conscious. I talked softly to him, laying my hand in his, and feeling the firm grip of his good hand squeeze my fingers. I could feel the hot tears that I had tried to keep in check, unsuccessfully, as they coursed down my cheeks. Looking at dad hooked up to a respirator, with all the other various tubes running in and out of him was more than I could stand.

My mother however, was already feeling as if my dad were getting more attention than was necessary and demanded that we all head down to the cafeteria for lunch. In short, SHE needed attention.

I had barely finished eating, when my mom made me so angry that I slammed my chair back, got up, and left. The effects of very little sleep, combined with her caustic comments were taking a toll, all because I had the audacity to ask questions about dad. She told me that I was not allowed to do that, because SHE is his wife, not me. It would be the first of many times, that I would have my patience tried by her in the weeks to come.

At 9 p.m., the heart surgeon came in with the devastating results of the tests they had taken on dad. There was nothing to soften this blow, as he bluntly began to discuss dad's health. He had suffered a thoracic aneurysm, which had started somewhere outside of the aorta. In short, he'd had a massive stroke.

The heart surgeon gave us very little time at all to come up with a decision on what was to be done about dad's condition. Plainly put, dad either had a very lengthy and risky surgery, having about a 5% chance of even surviving it, or he does not have it, and dies for sure, from a possible cough, sneeze, etc…. We had a couple of minutes to make up our minds. MY biggest worry was, if he DOES survive, what is his life going to be like? As before, though, I was not to ask any questions, so I sat back and kept my mouth shut. I was determined to try to support my mom's decision, even if I wasn't sure I agreed with it altogether.

The decision was made to go ahead with the surgery. As they wheeled dad away, I wondered if he had a chance at all, and why exactly we were putting him through all of this. I knew that I desperately needed some air and a change of scenery, so I walked to the chapel to pray. The floors were sticky, as they were getting ready to re-carpet, so I could not kneel, but I didn't care. I stood there for 10 minutes, praying aloud until I felt a sense of peace wash over me.

I just did not think dad was going to make it, and had mentally tried to prepare myself for the heartache that was sure to follow, but nine hours later, he was still alive. We were elated, and felt as if a miracle had just occurred. None of us realized that for dad especially, the nightmare had just begun.

Chapter 2: The Bittersweet Past

To understand the fierce love and loyalty I had, and will always have for my dad, the answers lie in my childhood.

Born on April 5, 1962 in Indianapolis, IN, I was the fourth and last child, born to a woman named Pam. Attractive and kind, she once again was unlucky in love, as she had been with the three other children's fathers, born out of wedlock. Stigmas were especially bad back then for a single woman with children and emotional problems, as well. Her childhood had been sad and lonely, with no real love ever given.

Growing up being told that her father walked out on her and her mother because of her birth, she neither knew how to deal with the men in her life, or how to find that love that each person so desperately desires. By the time she was 14 years of age, she had an obsessive-compulsive disorder that would include constant hand washing, and later, bulimia. She valiantly struggled with each child, trying to support them and keep them with her, but the only child she kept for the whole duration, was her first-born, who was five years older than I was.

At 18 months of age, I was a happy, chubby baby, who bounced in her crib constantly, unless I had an earache, which happened with regular frequency.

The pressure was growing from day to day from a specific child placement agency down in Indianapolis, for Pam to put me up for adoption. Since Pam did not work at all, and was on emotional disability, they made their case quite strong, until, finally, Pam handed me over.

Her oldest child still remembers being crouched in a closet, watching the social worker take me away. Soon after, my birthmother decided that she had made a mistake, and petitioned the court to get me back. By the time the hearing came about, I was already living in Northwest Indiana, with my soon-to-be adoptive parents. The judge took one look at my birthmother, and within the confines of his chambers, told her that she was "not at all what he had expected", and that he was very sorry, but when he went back out into the courtroom, he was going to rule against her. The adoption went through at record speed, becoming final five months later. Many people to this day still swear there was something very weird about that whole business, since adoptions can take a minimum of a year to go through, if all goes well. I was now two years old, and my life had totally changed.

Chapter 3: Welcome to my nightmare…

I can't remember not loving my dad. He was happy, and his gentle, easygoing ways drew people to him.

Daddy always had time for me, for as long as I can remember; how he did it, is beyond me. When I was two, he was already 46 years old, working long days as a route salesman for a well-known bread company. He got up at 3 a.m. everyday for work, many times not returning home until after 4 p.m. His arrival home was always the highlight of my day. I sometimes used to play hide and seek games with him, to make him find me when he got home. No matter how many times he played the same game, he would always act "surprised" when he would find me. I remember one particular game I played frequently with him. I would hide in his closet, where he always went to change his clothes when he got home. The closet had two sliding doors, and had little tabs that you could hang onto, and I used to hide in there, holding onto the tabs, so that when he would try to open the door, it wouldn't open, and then he would always say, "Gee, I can't get this door opened; it must be stuck." I would giggle in the darkness, letting him struggle with it for a few seconds, and then I would let it open, falling out of the closet, as he laughed and rubbed my head.

As loving, kind, and gentle as my dad was, my mother was the exact opposite. I have always been convinced that she suffers from some sort of mental condition. For years, I thought it to be manic-depression, because one never knew from minute to minute what to expect out of her. In recent years, I have become convinced that she is schizophrenic, because her sense of reality is distorted, to say the least.

She could go from being sweet to beating the snot out of me in the course of 30 seconds, and of course, it was over something so trivial, that no one normally would get upset about. Whenever anything at all went wrong in her world, it was always my fault.

She picked at everything I did or said, imagined slights of all types, and beat me daily, because she thought I was looking at her the wrong way. Because she seemed to have an outgoing personality, people found her quite engaging initially, but the longer they knew her, the less they liked her, until finally they just couldn't stand to be around her anymore. A total egomaniac, everything always revolved around her, and no one was entitled to his or her own opinions if they conflicted with hers, not even my dad. I had always wondered, from the time I was a child, how someone so wonderful got involved with someone like her. She never seemed to get along with anyone, not even her own mom and sister when they were alive, for very long.

From the time I was seven years old, I started going fishing with my dad at the resort we frequented every August in Michigan. Early in the morning, I would wake dad up, telling him that it was time to go fishing. Upon filling my pockets with little snacks for us, dad and I would grab our gear and head down to the pier.

After dad rowed out far enough, I would always watch him start the motor, and the Evinrude would come to life, with a roar. There was always such a thrill to that feeling of skimming along that lake, in those early hours of the morning, feeling the water splash up at me. When we would be skimming along that water as fast as we could go, dad and I would look at each other and smile. We always sat out in the boat in the middle of the lake, many times enjoying the sunrise in silence. Some days, we talked quite a bit, but other times, we were both quiet, but always enjoyed ourselves, nevertheless. I never had to worry about dad beating me, or suddenly getting so mad and flying off into a rage, and his kind, gentle nature was a natural, soothing balm, in a world that at times terrified me. Dad and I were out on the lake fishing, the day we heard the news of Elvis Presley's death on dad's little radio and we were both saddened and shocked by the news.

So many things that my mom did to me never did make any sense. I had started taking piano lessons at the age of seven, and God seemed to have given me some natural talent. I took lessons for 7 years, until my teacher told my mom that she had done all she could with me, and she referred my mom to a few professors. Back then, in the mid 70's, these guys already were charging $25/per half hour session, which was a lot of money back then.

Mondays were always piano lessons day, but they became something I feared and dreaded, because I was alone at home with my mom for dinner. She would have it prepared, and put a plate in front of me, and sit next to me, watching how I brought up the forkful of food to my mouth. If she did not like the way I did it, she slapped me across the face. Unfortunately, she never liked the way I did it, so with every bite I took, I was slapped. My nerves were shot by the time I got to piano lessons.

My piano teacher was a beautiful woman, inside and out, who often suspected that things were not right, but back then, people just did not get involved. She was a widow, and on occasion, she asked me to play "Harbor Lights," an old song that both she and her late husband had loved. I remember always seeing a few tears in her eyes when I would play it for her.

She made a living out of giving piano and organ lessons in her home, and I loved her dearly. She always made me feel very safe and loved in that half-hour, away from my mom, in her music studio. I hated to see that time end, but by the time I would get home, my father would be there, and my mom's physical abuse at least, would end. However, if I even remotely looked like I had been crying when piano lessons ended, my mother would pop me several times in the face on the drive home, while she screamed at me. She never hit me when my dad was around. The verbal abuse was still there, but then, she verbally abused him too. It seemed to be just part of her everyday life, to make other people unbearably miserable.

I remember one particular incident when I was eleven years old when my mom flew off into one of her nastier rages and backed me into the corner of the living room door. There, she repeatedly kicked and slapped me, until suddenly, my nerves went out on me, and I shook violently from head to toe. I remember thinking that I must have bad nerves. After that hour of hell, she took me to children's choir at our church, where I spent the next hour shaking nonstop.

The verbal abuse never DID end; it just continued, on into my teens, when I grew angry inside. Angry with the mother I was stuck with, who, by that time, I started to really hate, at times. Angry that she was a control freak, who hated all of my friends, and controlled every aspect of my life that she could. And angry that all of my friends were out having fun, and being kids, but I was stuck at home cleaning my mom's house, and at her constant beck and call.

I grew up in Gary, when it was a neat place to live. I had always loved school, and the added bonus of having to be away from my mom for several hours, but my school life was filled with pain and ridicule as well.

My mother would buy clothes that no one else had even thought of wearing, and when she purchased them at Marshall Fields', that automatically meant that you wore them at least once a week, no matter how much you hated it, or how much abuse you took at school every time you wore it.

I remember one outfit that she had purchased at Marshall Fields. It was a heavy flannel tweed material, the top was like a buttoned down jacket, and the pants were actually, what they called "knickers" back then. They buttoned around the knees, and every week I dreaded having to wear that outfit, as the teasing and ridicule seemed to go on forever. When I would try to tell my mom what I had to deal with all day at school, she would, of course, get extremely angry, cursing and slapping me at times, for the ungracious person she thought that I was. Other times, she did not get as angry, but would say that she does not care about other kids, and is not supporting them, and then quote me the old sticks and stones verse.

After I had finished 8th grade, we moved out of Gary about 12 miles east to a different town. My freshman year was another nerve-wracking time, as I was trying to make friends, and fit in as best as I could. My mother always had me looking as plain as possible. She made me wear my hair short, and whenever I would grow it out long, she would use it to grab me whenever she flew off into one of her still-many rages. Make-up was not allowed, even in high school, and she controlled my life as much as she possibly could.

The summer that we moved out of Gary, I still had my hair long. My scalp was aching from the abuse it took earlier of having her yank on it while she hit me. By then, I grew to my full height of 5'9", and this woman was a whole 5 ft. tall, but it never stopped her or slowed her down in the least.

She took off one afternoon, like a witch on wheels, having beat me good just moments before. She decided to run over to the new house we were moving into, and had left a cigarette lying in the ashtray. What lured me to it I will never know, but I picked it up, lit and smoked it, as though I was an old pro at it. No coughing, no feeling sick. Just pure relaxation.

That summer was pure hell. By the time school started, I did not know what I dreaded the most; starting a new school, or being around my mother, whose rages only seemed to get worse the older I got. All that summer, she was yanking my hair, and beating me pretty much everyday.

One day she got it in her head that she hated my hair long, so without any warning, she took me to a salon and had them cut all my hair off, so that now I felt like I was starting a new school looking like a geek, as well.

By the time school actually got into full swing, I enjoyed a couple cigarettes a day, on the sly, of course. It became something I really enjoyed and looked forward to, in a world where I did not look forward to much.

I did manage to make friends and acquaintances. Some smoked cigarettes, and were developing a bit of an attitude. Of course, all my friends learned about my life at home, and everyone was always shocked by the madness I endured everyday.

Phone calls were torturous, also. Inevitably, I would get phone calls and my mother stood right on top of me during the entire call, which lasted 5 minutes if I was real lucky, and my mom was in a good mood. If five minutes went by and I was still talking, all hell broke loose. Sometimes a beating followed, and sometimes it didn't, but either way, the caller quickly came to hate my mother as well.

In my sophomore year, I had straight, very short hair, since that is what my mother demanded, and one day she decided I needed a trim. She gave me the money that I needed, and after school I went to the beauty shop and had it trimmed. I walked straight home from there, which was only about three blocks.

After dinner, dad went bowling on his league, and my mother flew into one of her more violent rages. She started screaming at me about what a liar I was, and that I really had not stopped and gotten a haircut. According to her, I had spent the money on something else. I could tell that she was way off, even for her, and I knew that it would be worse than usual this time. In a fit of rage, even after I begged her to call the hairdresser and ask her if she had trimmed my hair, she got out her sewing box, found her scissors, and proceeded to take random swipes at my hair. "There," she said, the rage finally subsiding,

"now you finally look like you have a haircut. And don't you ever try to lie to me again, you worthless piece of shit."

Needless to say, at 15 I was devastated after I looked in the mirror. It wasn't as bad as I thought it would be, but it was very short now, and I already was suffering from low self-esteem, when it came to my physical appearance.

I told a couple of my friends about it the next day, but I never did tell my dad about it. I never told him about half of the stuff that went on, unfortunately. Looking back on it, I think I should have been more assertive, but I was warned over and over "not to go running to your father." I was terrified of her when she was in the middle of one of her rages, so I usually never did tell my dad about the things she would do. There were times I really thought she would end up killing me one day.

There were times that some major fights broke out over me, because my dad knew of the verbal abuse, anyway. To this day, though, I don't believe he truly knew how sick this woman was.

Soon before my 16th birthday, I went across the street, to a neighbor's house, to give her a piano lesson. While I was gone, my mother decided to play junior detective and go through my purse, my closets, drawers, and anything else that was in my room. Nothing was ever personal or private in that house, ever. She found four cigarettes in the pocket of my purse, and a jar of liquid paper for typing class.

Upon returning home, I walked into the foyer to see her standing at the top of the stairs already working on yet another tirade, asking me, "What are these?" Getting older, and ever more tired of her nonstop rages and abuse, I also started to assert myself more.

I knew I would get beat, but something inside me was growing weary of it all, and I was starting to grow up. "You should know; you smoke them too," I smirked.

Next, she thrust the bottle of liquid typing paper right under my nose, and was convinced that I was sniffing it. The whole idea of sniffing liquid paper unfortunately struck me as funny. Thankfully, my dad was home too, but said nothing, watching the scene intently. My mother flew into a rage then, and slapped me as I came up the stairs, and then her and my dad got into it.

Dinnertime was tedious, and did not bode well for the digestive tract, as usual. The dinner hour was usually hard to take in general, just because my mother liked to use that time to complain and pick on me. This meal was worse, because she used the time to rail on me the entire meal about smoking cigarettes, pausing once in awhile, ironically, to light one for herself.

In a flash of anger, she jumped out of her seat, and announced to dad that he needed to "talk to me." As I cleared the dinner table and carried the dishes to the sink, my dad told me to leave them, and come sit down at the table with him. I did, taking my usual seat across from him. He motioned for me to lean closer, conspiratorially casting furtive glances from side to side, as my mother was sitting, listening, and waiting in the very next room. Once again he motioned, then told me to lean closer, and I did, once again, and so did he. Leaning as close to each other as we could, without getting out of our seats, my dad asked me, "Why didn't you hide them better?" To which my mother promptly leapt out of her chair, and bounded back into the kitchen, yelling, "That's not what I meant by talking to her."

My dad just laughed, and then told my mom to relax; it was no big deal. As far as he was concerned, I was not into drugs or alcohol, and cigarettes, growing up in the late 70's, seemed a small price to pay.

About the time that my smoky little secret was discovered, I went with my dad one Thursday night, for his bowling league, and was a bit amazed when he reached into his glove compartment, pulled out a cigar, unwrapped it, lit it, and then looked at me with a grin. I asked him when he had started to smoke again, as he had given it up for years, and he told me he had just started a couple months before again. He asked me not to say anything to my mom, and of course, I didn't. Her rages seemed to include him with decent regularity, and the constant bickering and yelling she made as a way of life in our home, drove my dad and I nuts, at times. He told me that I could smoke a cigarette around him if I wanted to, and that that would be just fine with him. For months, it remained our secret.

My mom stayed mad for weeks when she demanded that I swear on the Holy Bible that I would never smoke again, and I refused. She followed me all about the house with her Bible, and into the bathroom even.

Months later, finally, my mother discovered my father's return to cigars, and as predicted, went totally ballistic, and then asked me if I knew about this, right in front of my dad. I just shook my head, and told her no. I sure wasn't going to tell her anything about my dad. He was my friend, and the only other person in the house that showed any signs of sanity.

Many times when she was angry in general, she would take it out on me, and tell me that I was such a disappointment, and that she wished that she had never adopted me. When I was 17, I remember telling her one night after she'd said that to me that I wished she hadn't, either.

The last time that she really went off on me bad, and physically came after me, I was 19. I was working two jobs, and going to school a couple nights a week. She was already angry, because she had discovered that I was still very close to an elderly couple that I had absolutely adored since childhood. They had never been blessed with children of their own, but I just loved being with them, and soaked up every ounce of love and kindness they gave me, whenever I went over there. It was always like a ray of sunshine, in a world of darkness, to be around people that actually thought I was sweet, fun, and great. Things I never heard at all at home. Once a month or so, I would skip class at college, and go visit them, just to check on them and see how they were doing. It was a political science class, and the lectures were unbelievably boring, but I always seemed to get A's on my tests, so I rationalized cutting class a couple of times a month easily. Plus, because I did not want to go to business school, my mother refused to help at all financially, with any schooling past high school. I figured that since I was paying for my own schooling, I could cut class once in awhile, if I wanted to. Back then, I was a psychology major, thinking seriously about a career in social work, but after a year, I dropped out of college.

After a 10 day stay in the hospital, in 1981, from gall bladder surgery, my mother came home, and I had the whole house to run, because, "I am post-op, and can't do anything", she would say to me.

One night, after I had finished doing the dishes, and put all the laundry away, a friend called, who now lived in Arizona. We had been close all through high school. After two or three minutes of chatting about the new horse she had just gotten, my mother started screaming at me from the basement to get off of the phone. I put my hand over the phone, and told her that I just got on, and would be finishing up in a few minutes, as I had not talked to this friend in several weeks. She continued to scream at me, in the lower level of the bi-level, and finally came tearing up the stairs, right after I had hung up the phone. My dad was bowling that night, so he wasn't home. I had thought at the time, that she sure ran up those stairs pretty fast, for someone who was so sick, and "post-operative", as she liked to tell me a thousand times a day. She immediately wanted to know what me and that "whore" were talking about. I politely told her that we were talking about her new horse that she had just gotten, and she wanted to tell me all about her. My mother told me that she did not believe me, that I was a liar, and would always be a liar, and then proceeded to ask me again what we were talking about. Finally, I was getting very angry, and in a burst of temper myself, told her that it really wasn't any of her damned business what we were talking about, since she did not want to believe the truth. Quick as a flash, she came over and followed me around the coffee table, beating me across the face and back, whenever she could get close enough to me.

By the time her rage finally subsided, I went to bed with a very sore back. I knew that I would have to get up in the morning and go to work. By the next morning, my back was in major pain, and I spent the day where I worked answering the phones for a commodity brokerage, in massive pain. The longer I was in pain, the angrier I became.

When I got home that night, both of my parents were sitting in the living room, reading the newspaper. I walked in and announced in front of both of them, that the next time my mother laid so much as a finger on me, I was going to call the cops and have her thrown in jail where she belonged. With that, I turned on my heel and left the room. I heard my mom then, making up her usual lies when my dad questioned her. An argument ensued, but nothing more was ever said about it.

A few months before I turned 21, I met John. He was working at a gas station in town, and we started dating. At first, my mother liked him, but then, just a couple short months later, they were both at complete odds with each other, and for the next two years, he never came in the house when he picked me up. It was not until three months before we got married, that he came back in the house and apologized, however grudgingly, to her. Not that I blamed him. He was apologizing for something that he did not do, which was so typical where my mom was concerned. Everything was always about her, and what she wanted. A person had to constantly stroke her ego, and if you did not do exactly what she wanted, she turned on you, like a cobra.

As every week passed, my nerves grew worse and worse. I laughed nervously of just eloping and getting away from all of the pressure.

The summer before, I was diagnosed with irritable bowel syndrome, a disease that has a lot to do with stress. My colon had been balking for months, with the stress I endured. My mother had to have everything her way, even where my gown was concerned. I did not pick out my own gown; I was told what I would be wearing.

I just did not stand up to her back then, the way I would in later years. My mother went ballistic upon finding out that my mother-in-law- to- be came in the bridal shop where we bought my dress and asked the clerk to show it to her. The clerk supposedly would not show it to her, per my mother's orders, which caused a big fight between my soon-to-be husband and I.

Another fight ensued over my mother-in-law saying that I had to use the same knife to cut the cake as her other daughter-in-law and a couple other family members had used. I had told her that my mom had already bought one and had it engraved. Once again, I was stuck in the middle. It always felt like someone was always going to be mad, no matter what we did. By the time we got into the last month before the wedding, I think we both were ready to just elope. I was sick and tired of playing monkey in the middle, too. But I was just getting started.

I sweated through the rehearsal dinner, as my mother was convinced that my husband's family was no good. They had not followed protocol to a tee, meaning, they did not do things the way she wanted them done. Nor had they stroked her ego enough, so she immediately took an intense dislike to them, setting the stage for major problems down the road. Holidays were a tug-of-war match that I could never win.

The dinner went as well as it could, with my mother's caustic comments kept down to a low roar, which was as good as it could get for her. My dad of course, got along with everyone and was very congenial and well mannered, but my mom always had her own agenda and rules that applied only to her.

She started mellowing out more, the last few days before the wedding, because she really had no choice by then, and my dad was not working much that week either.

Daddy had retired from the bakery in 1981, when I was 19, and had exactly one week to enjoy retirement, before my mother had another job lined up for him. He worked part-time at Kmart, and did very well there, as his personality worked in his favor for sales in the appliance department.

Even after I was busy working, dating, and doing what most people in their early 20's do, dad still always looked out for me.

Because he was not allowed to smoke his cigars in the house, he had to go hang out in the garage, whenever he wanted to smoke. He always kept a close eye on my car. I never had to worry about being low on washer fluid, or anything else, for that matter. When the oil started looking bad, he advised me to get an oil change.

I had a habit of drinking a beer on the way home from the law firm I had been working for at the time. I worked 4:30-11:30, and my mother was usually asleep in her chair when I got home. I was never allowed to stay up and watch TV, or use the blow-dryer on my hair after a shower, etc., because it used up too much electricity, so I had to come home and go straight to bed. Even in my early 20's, I had to be in by midnight, and never could stay out any later, even though I paid $100 in rent a month, paid the water bill, and did all of the housework. I never had privileges, because my mother had to have complete control over me whenever she possibly could. So on the trip home to unwind and relax after a night at work, I would drink a beer. I would get on the expressway and be home from work in 20-25 minutes.

Dad found about six empty beer bottles one day, hidden under the seat, and told me simply that that was not a good idea, because if I was pulled over, it could get ugly. He removed them, and asked me not to keep empty beer bottles in the car anymore.

One day, dad took me over to a local tire dealer, and we got the tires changed and rotated. About a month later, as I drove to work, a horrible sound that sounded like a machine gun kept me company for the whole drive. That night, I called Dad and told him about it, and he told me that he would be outside listening, as I came down the street when I got home. We could not see much in the dark, but dad's face looked grim, and he told me that I would not be driving that car anymore, until we took it in and found out exactly what was wrong.

The next morning, we took it over to the place that we had been to before, and upon fixing the car for me, the man that had worked on it that day and before, came out and talked to us for a bit. He told us that someone had loosened every tire to the point that they would have just fallen off if I would have drove the car another day. At 80 mph, that would have been disastrous. From that point on, dad made it a habit of checking the tires well, too. But then again, Dad always took real good care of me.

My husband and I got married on August 30, 1985, and dad walked me down the aisle. We had all taken many pictures, and dad and I had laughed and joked for most of the time. When the organist started to play, signaling the ceremony was about to begin, I suddenly started to shake uncontrollably. Dad teased me, and asked if I was sure this was what I wanted. When I had assured him that it was, he patted my hand and told me that it would be okay. As we started down the aisle together, dad looked somber, which was rare for him. At one point, he almost looked as though he had tears in his eyes. I am sure that he did, actually. It's like we both knew that our lives would be very different from here on, but I knew that I would always be his girl forever.

Chapter 4: The abuse continues….

The early years of marriage were happy and good, except when it came time for the holidays, or if more than a couple of weeks went by and I did not come out for a visit. We lived an hour and a half away, and both of us worked full-time all week long. After the first 6 months of marriage, we moved to a different town, a bit further away, but closer to where my husband worked.

My mother would always offer to let us borrow money for big things, such as when we purchased our mobile home in 1986, but I never wanted to accept money from her, because I knew the strings attached to it would be more than I could stand. There was also a certain amount of pride with us, in wanting to take care of things ourselves.

Sometimes we would go a few months and everything would be decent. My mom seemed to have accepted the marriage and approved of our new purchase, but one always was very guarded around her, walking around on eggshells, and never knowing exactly what would set her off, once again. Because, inevitably, something ALWAYS did.

She has always been the only person I know, who could take a simple sentence, and twist it into something very different, taking complete offense to it, too, of course. Then, she would mull things over in her mind with her new "story" until she would swear that things happened that way, no matter how many people told her that it didn't. The absolute worst, is when you are right there with her, and she tells you something, and then a week or two later, she tells you the exact opposite. This happened so often, but one incident, especially, sticks out in my mind.

One of dad's sisters' got very ill with cancer, in 1988, and was laying in the hospital, dying. Until he had met my mother, my dad and her were very close, as they were close in age as well. She told the family whenever they would come up and visit her, that she desperately wanted to see dad before she died, and word got to my parents that she was dying, and wanted to see him. One day, while he was working his job at K-mart, my mom told John and I that she told my dad that if he even thought about seeing his sister, that upon his return home, the locks would be changed, and all of his stuff would be laying out on the front lawn. She held a 30- year grudge with this sister over something that she "supposedly" heard her say. To this day, I have no idea if dad ever DID see her before she died.

Earlier in January of 1988, my mom had been diagnosed with lymphoma, and called to tell me the news. I listened carefully, trying to be supportive, when quite suddenly, she began to rage at me. After calling me every name she could think of, she let me know that this latest problem of hers was all my fault, from all the years of stress I had caused her. In her mind, this was God's way of punishing me, for the horrible person I had always been.

I said goodbye and slammed the phone down, hurling it across the room. When I talked to her the next time, about a week later, she seemed oblivious to anything she had said the previous week. She asked me what I had expected, her getting such awful news like that. She said that she felt a need to lash out and yell at someone, and that I should be able to understand that. In short, I needed to just grow up and accept it.

Meantime, dad seemed to get mellower with time. Our personalities grew a bit more different, the older we both got. Dad seemed so resigned, and the old fight in him seemed to just disappear. My brother, sister, and I all saw signs of brainwashing that would probably teach the KGB a new trick or two. Dad never complained, but then again, that seemed to be his style.

Dad and I enjoyed playing outdoor jarts together. When we would go over there to visit, we would get those jarts out and play a few games. Dad seemed to kick my butt, nine times out of ten, and tease me with his gentle laugh. At times, we would be neck and neck until the game was almost over, and dad would win. He seemed to love those games, especially, and enjoyed watching me try to beat him. When he would win, he would chuckle, and comment on what a close game it was.

Inevitably, my mom always came out, almost immediately, as though the paranoid side of her couldn't stand to miss something.

One day, my mom had been particularly ugly to dad, yelling at him and calling him a stupid jackass, the way she always did. As time went on, she seemed to have him do more and more chores around the house, too. I asked him how and why he puts up with being yelled at and treated so badly, and he just shrugged his shoulders and said, "that is just the way your mother is."

Many times, he seemed to give me that answer, as though there was no other explanation. This particular time, though, he also mentioned that it did no good getting into it with her, because he would be hearing about it long after I went back home. I could definitely understand that.

Unfortunately, my mother didn't confine the name-calling and verbal abuse to just our home. In many cases, public humiliation was a way of life as well.

Five weeks before John and I got married, my sister and her husband celebrated their 25th wedding anniversary at the club that they belonged to, with 200 + guests. Sitting at a table, enjoying a drink with another couple, the laughter froze on my lips, and everyone else's, when suddenly my mother began shouting across the large room.

"Damn it, get over here, you stupid jackass." Unfortunately, she felt the need to repeat this infamous line a couple more times, in the unlikely event, that someone in the room might actually have missed it the first time.

My dad took it all in stride, of course. My soon-to-be husband was horrified, and leaned over to speak to me.

"If you EVER do that to me…" he said, letting the sentence trail off into the sunset. I shook my head, still recovering from the embarrassment of my mother's words. The room was just now starting to buzz with noise, once again. The old saying of hearing a pin drop, buzzed in my brain, and I felt like I was in the middle of a popular TV commercial where the room went totally silent.

A couple weeks after my mom told us what she told dad about visiting his dying sister, the poor woman passed away, and my mom sat there and told John and I, that "she tried to get him to go visit his sister before she died, but he just wouldn't do it, because if ANYONE hurts her at all, he won't have anything to do with them." John and I just sat there, looking at each other, and then looking at her. A look of total disbelief passed through his eyes, because at that point, he finally understood what I had been saying about her for years.

Three nights before Mother's Day in 1987, I suffered quite a muscle spasm in my back, to the point that John had to take me to the emergency room. I couldn't even stand up. The doctor put me on four days of bed rest and muscle relaxers. I got up for a few minutes to let our dog out and then remembered that Mother's Day was in two days, so I ordered a beautiful bouquet of flowers to be sent out to my mom. On Saturday, she called me to tell me that the flowers were beautiful, but why didn't I just bring them with me when I came in. I reminded her that I was on absolute bed rest all weekend, and then all hell broke loose. She raged and yelled at me, telling me what a miserable excuse of a daughter I was, after all she'd sacrificed and done for me all these years. It droned on and on, until I got tired of listening to her and said goodbye.

Like a dummy, I got in the car on Monday, and drove out there to see her. The first 10 minutes I was there, she literally cussed me out and screamed at me, again, about the miserable excuse of a daughter that I am. I was not even supposed to be out of bed yet, but she didn't care. After awhile, she cooled down, and I left a couple hours later. As I got onto the toll road to head home, first my right arm, and then my left arm, started tingling very strangely, and then a crushing, heavy feeling on my chest that made breathing difficult. I drove on, becoming more freaked out by what all was happening to me. I swore I was having a heart attack, and alternated between praying and breathing in a brown bag.

Halfway home, I stopped at a rest area to call my husband and tell him what was going on, and told him that if I wasn't home in 45 minutes or so, to call the county police to come look for me. That incident marked the second full-blown panic attack I'd had. Too much stress for too many years had finally come to a head.

I finally arrived home, and was never so thankful to be there. Unfortunately, in years to come, I would experience most of my panic attacks while I was driving or riding. I struggled with the anxiety on my own, until a friend encouraged me to get the help I needed.

I now understood that years upon years of stress take a toll on the body. My mother never did grasp that concept, though. When my children were small, she expected me to come out every Saturday, without my husband or the kids and visit her, whenever she was lonely, not feeling well, or whatever.

I decided to be honest with her and tell her about the panic attacks. I didn't expect sympathy, but had hoped for a little understanding. Instead, I was informed that only a complete nutcase would be talking about these things, and had me all but committed.

Next, she tried the theory that I am just a liar. Either way, I now was quite furious, and took out my bad temper on the telephone, hurling it across the room. For the millionth time, I felt like I could so easily walk away from my mom, and never see her again, and that would be fine with me. But then, there was always the fact that I would probably never see my dad again, either, if I did that. That just wasn't an option for me.

Chapter 5: and then, there were three.

In August of 1989, I found out I was pregnant, and was as excited as I could possibly be. Dad was delighted too; I could see the joy in his eyes when we would talk about the baby that was to come. He never cared if the baby was a boy or girl, but many of us had a hunch it would be a boy. The due date was set for April 15, 1990, which was Easter Sunday that year, but I was nowhere near ready to deliver, even though I felt like the Goodyear blimp by then, and had quit working at the end of March. I had wanted two weeks off before the baby came, just to rest and make sure that everything was in order, but I ended up with a month off, instead.

My parents were in Hawaii, when our firstborn, a son, was born. He weighed in at 9lb., and 2oz., and 23 inches long. He was a bit jaundiced, so he came into the world with the look of a suntan, and the most beautiful face. He had none of the wrinkly, blotchy look about him that many babies do, because he was later in making his entry into the world.

Three days later, at home, after having a c-section, my mother called from Hawaii, and sounded as though she was crying because she was out there, instead of back in Indiana, checking out her new grandson; her first REAL grandson, as she would tell my sister.

Five months earlier, at Christmastime, my mother informed my dad's daughter that since she was soon expecting her first "real" grandchild, she would not be coming over for Christmas, as I was not feeling well, and did not want to do a lot of extra driving. My mother said many hateful things to her, and for the next ten years, the relationship between those two was over. My mother of course, did nothing wrong, and gave a very different version of the story when questioned.

My sister's children had nothing more to do with my parents after that either. Dad appeared to put it all out of his mind, and seemed oblivious to it all, at times. My mother had deep-seated anger and issues with my dad's kids, especially his son, even though he had never even been a part of the Christmas exchange of words or anything else, for that matter. For the next ten years, all I ever heard, was that if anything ever happened to dad, she would make sure that his son would be barred from the funeral. Venom seemed to spew from her lips, at the mere mention of his name.

Even though my mother usually had only negative things to say about us having a baby, she seemed delighted when she saw him, but it was not long at all before she was constantly telling me what to do, and what she thought I was doing wrong with the baby. Mostly, she accused me of loving the baby too much, holding him too much, and not putting him in the crib and just letting him cry. She felt that I gave him too much attention.

"So what if he cries," she would say. "You need to let him know who's the boss; just let him cry" and many other assorted comments. It always galled her that I never paid any attention to any of those comments. He was MY child, and I wanted to do what I felt was right. Although I never said it to her, I felt like she was the last person on earth that should be giving advice about how to raise a child.

As the baby grew older, she came to resent the time I spent with him, because in her mind, it took me away from time I should be spending with her. However, the older I was getting, I was starting to lay down my own rules, and getting better at sticking with them. There was always hell to pay when I stood up to her but I was getting tired of the intimidation.

When my son started walking and getting very mobile, Grandpa found it amusing but my mom did not. Whenever he would get a foot away from anything, she would start yelling at him not to touch. I quickly got to the point where I hated going over there, just because she was always yelling at my son, and I ended up a nervous wreck.

It was easier all the way around when they came over to our house, because my mother seemed more relaxed, not worrying about her furniture, her rugs, etc. The minute he would begin to fuss at all, she wanted him down for a nap. My mother's idea of a good baby was one who never cried, fussed, or did much of anything at all.

Chapter 6: And last, but not least...

Two days before Mother's Day, in May of 1992, I found out I was pregnant again, and I was elated. I was very ready to have another baby, now that we had sold our mobile home, and gotten into a house. On Mother's Day, we were all in the car, heading to a restaurant, and my dad was driving, when I told my mom the happy news. But she had nothing positive to say about it. She seemed determined to spread gloom and doom everywhere she was. I never heard positive things from her, and in the absolute joy of discovering that I would have another baby, I was not amused by any of her comments, and I told her so. My dad remained quiet, for the most part, but did mention that she should just let me be happy. That seemed to be all he ever wanted for me; at least he seemed excited to become a grandpa again.

My pregnancy seemed uneventful, as did the first, and that year, we went in to see our families the week before Christmas because the baby was going to be taken by c-section on Jan. 8, when I was 39 weeks along. The doctor was adamant that he did not want to take a chance of me going into labor, or of letting the baby get too big.

That week of Christmas, I was talking to my dad on the phone for a few minutes, and I asked him what he wanted for Christmas. He told me a beautiful baby girl. Two weeks later, Grandpa got his wish.

This time, my parents decided that they were going to be at the hospital when this baby was born, and when I was back in my room, both of my parents were there too. My mother was telling me that my daughter was not amused with the bath and hair washing that she had received and had protested with screams the whole time. When the nurses brought her to me, she was a perfect little angel who was decidedly hungry. We marveled at her long, slim fingers, so much like mine. Dad was grinning from ear to ear, as he looked at this newest grandbaby of his. After having lunch in the cafeteria with John, they headed back home.

Chapter 7: The kids are growing up

Dad proved to be a wonderful grandpa, as I knew he would be. He delighted in bouncing babies on his knee, and coaxing them out of an occasional bad mood. My mother, however, seemed to only tell them constantly what they were doing wrong in her opinion, and could never just relax and let them be. She spent much of the time either telling my kids what they were doing wrong, or telling me all the things I was doing wrong in raising them.

When my daughter was only three months old, my husband's paternal grandparents both died, within 5 days of each other. We went to the visitation when his grandmother passed away, and after a few hours, he brought us back to my parents' house. They would take us back to the hotel a bit later, so that he could go back to the funeral parlor to be with his family.

My son was coloring quietly, which is all my kids were ever allowed to do, and the baby, who was three months old, was lying on the couch. The modular home my parents lived in was a two-bedroom, with a bit of an open concept from part of the living room to the dining room and the kitchen. I had gone into the kitchen to get a glass of water, and as I was drinking it, I could see my mother holding a cigarette with a hot ash hanging as she bent over my daughter, and a split second later, my baby was screaming like I had never heard anyone scream before.

I flew out of that kitchen, and immediately picked her up to see an angry red splotch on her face, just inches away from her right eye, as the result of the hot ash that had fallen on her. I was livid. I asked my mother what she was thinking, bending over a baby with a lit cigarette in her mouth.

She looked me right in the eye, and told me that that was just a pimple, not a burn, and that she had not had the cigarette in her mouth. A mixture of unleashed anger and total disbelief coursed through my body. I knew that I had seen her hastily put the cigarette down in the ashtray as soon as the baby started screaming. The fact that she had lied about it only enraged me further, because I told her that I had seen the whole thing. But of course in her sick mind, I only THOUGHT I saw what I had seen. I finally let it go, because I could see that she was never going to admit what she had done. I never forgot the incident, though, because it proved yet again that she could not distinguish the truth from the lies.

As the children grew, my mother always had "workbooks" for the kids to do. Pretending to be the teacher, she analyzed everything, even my two-year-old daughter coloring outside of the lines. A lot of what my kids had to put up with, only served as a reminder of my own childhood. An A- should have been an A, or an A+. Nothing I did was ever good enough.

Chapter 8: Moving Away

When we announced that we were possibly moving to Texas, my mother tried everything she could possibly think of to dissuade us from going, but in October of 1997, we moved to Texas, anyways. A huge part of me was so excited. I was ready to move away, and begin a new life. I knew I would miss my dad terribly, and I did worry sometimes about both of them, because I knew they were getting up in years, but I also knew it was time for me to start living my own life, and be away from so many of the frustrations I had had for so many years. Two days before we left, my parents drove out to say goodbye, and my mother bawled like a baby. I had never seen her cry that much, and there were tears in my dad's eyes, as he hugged me fiercely.

It was sad and painful to say goodbye to them, but I was still very excited about starting a new life.

A year later, they came out to visit for three days. I never understood why they went to the trouble of flying out, and then be in such a hurry to get back home, but my mother was a volunteer for Meals on Wheels by then, and claimed that she needed to get back two days before she had to work, so she would be able to rest. I had not seen them for a year, and suddenly they both seemed to have really aged. My dad was now walking hunched over a bit, and his hair was now completely white. My mother moved very slowly from hip pain.

The visit went okay, for the most part, although at one point I got furious with my mother. We went out to eat on the last day they were in TX, and she picked at my son constantly. She was never capable of treating both of the kids nicely. During the entire visit, she treated my daughter like gold, and picked on my son constantly. The kids were seven and four at the time, and finally during dinner, I told her that that was enough. I hated seeing kids get so upset at dinner. We were out in a restaurant, and my son was getting furious, not that I blamed him. When he got older, he would get better at holding his tongue, but at that age, he still hadn't learned how to just ignore her yet.

As were her rules, poor dad would stay up watching a TV show with us, trying to stay awake and failing miserably, so that my mom could go to bed first. He then had to wait at least a half hour before he could go to bed, because he supposedly snored, and she needed to be asleep before he went to bed. When we would put the kids to bed every night, he would come in their rooms and pray with us, and kiss them goodnight. It was my turn to hug dad fiercely this time, wondering when I would see them both again. I cried when the car left the driveway, because they suddenly seemed so old. My dad was so quiet, almost lost in his own world, and there seemed to be sadness about him as well.

Chapter 9: The Long Road Home

Coming back to Indiana was the last thing in the world that I had wanted. The warm weather and sunny days seemed to be soothing to my soul, and even though my marriage was very strained at times, I had never been happier, for the most part. The thought of coming back to long winters, and all the family problems for me that went along with my life in Indiana seemed like a nightmare, and try though I might, I could not seem to let go.

I had found the warmth in friendships, and a spiritual life out there that lifted me up, higher than I had ever been lifted up before. In many ways, I had finally come into my own out there, free to break away from the things that had held me back for so long. I thrived in my new environment, and was embraced by the two church families I had come to know and love. I played the piano for both churches; one that I belonged to, and one that I stumbled upon through a help wanted ad.

The people there were without a trace of arrogance, and though a lot of them were far from rich in money and material things, they had truly found the kingdom of God, in every way that mattered. On my last day there, the party that was thrown for me was beyond anything I could have imagined. Roses, a beautiful bible, and a plaque that someone had made for me, were just some of the items I was given, plus cake and ice cream, held in my honor. I cried all the way home, feeling as though my heart was forever broken. Little did I know, it would break more.

I watched helplessly, almost detached in some ways, as the home I so dearly loved was emptied. When it was completely empty, I could not bear to stay in it any longer. As I walked out of my home for the last time, I felt as though I had left a part of me behind. I wanted to be positive about this move back up north, but the thought of everything going back to the way it was before, was unthinkable for me. A nightmare that I did not want to relive again.

On October 8, 1999, we got back into Indiana, and stopped off at my parents' house for a bit to say hello. The reunion went quite well, and I was glad to see my parents, especially dad. I never totally realized how much I missed him, until I saw him again. Never in my wildest dreams would it have occurred to me, that exactly one year later, I would never see him again.

Chapter 10: Reality bites

I got a job right away. Working evenings, some days, and weekends, I was plunged into the fickle world of retail, where some days were certainly better than others. I learned a lot about people. The job itself wasn't bad, but the pay stunk.

The whole time that I was working, and desperately trying to live my life, I struggled with the pain inside of me. I wasn't happy anymore, and didn't feel happy to be back. Friends were quite happy to have me back, but I knew that I had changed a lot in the two years that I had been gone. I tried to go back to the church that I had belonged to for the 11 years before we left for Texas, but even though I had friends and acquaintances there that I cherished, I just couldn't seem to get back in the groove there, and felt very much like an outsider.

I realized, yet again, that you could never go back. The sweet and meek people I had left behind were replaced in some ways by cynical, arrogant ones that insisted on their own way, and because I now knew better, I seemed to be looking for something else.

I continued to have the female problems I'd been plagued with, as well. In March of 2000, I prepared for a laparascopy, hysteroscopy, and a lumpectomy, in hopes of ridding myself of the heavy and painful menstrual periods I was having. Having dealt with the periods for four years already, I wanted answers and went to my old doctor to get some results. The lump in my lower left abdomen proved to be a mass of endometriosis. My doctor removed it, making a three- inch incision to get it out, because it was bigger than he had anticipated, and got rid of all of the scar tissue that he could.

My parents came out that weekend, and we had a relaxing afternoon visiting, although I was still in a bit of discomfort. I looked forward to my upcoming trip to Texas that I was taking the next month. It would be my first trip alone that I had taken in 18 years, and I needed the time away desperately. I blamed my husband for bringing me back up here, when I had not wanted to come back at all, and it was putting a lot of strain on our marriage. I looked forward to going out there, visiting with friends, and feeling God's presence at the beach, where I had always felt so happy. I also felt like I needed some closure to my life in Texas as well, since everything had happened so fast when we left. It would be the last time I saw my dad, whole and happy.

Chapter 11: Enjoy it while it lasts

All good things really DO end, I was soon to realize, and sometimes a lot sooner than you want them to. I had gotten out to Texas on April 15, and around midnight on April 17, my husband called to give me the shocking news about my father's stroke. Immediately, my mind started whirling about what I would do, who I would call, etc. My husband hated the thought of me having to cut my trip short, and told me not to make any flight changes until he had had a chance to get up there the following day to the hospital himself, to see how dad was doing. But the next morning, having barely slept at all, I called the airlines and had my flight changed. The only available flight on Tuesday was late at night, so I caught the first flight back on Wed. morning. I spent my last day in Texas with friends, at the beach.

As I sat on the beach, I felt calm and at peace, even though I didn't have a clue what I would face when I got back to Indiana. The beach had always had that effect on me, and it was always a place where I felt God's presence.

I felt calm and strengthened, having no idea how badly I would need that strength in the weeks and months to come.

Chapter 12: Life after the stroke…. but not for Dad

After he had had the surgery on April 19, it was several days before he really came out of it, and it scared us all. I worried mostly about brain damage and what his life would be like if he ever came out of it. Approximately ten days later, he finally did come out of it, slowly, but surely. More tests, more speculation. As time went by, I seriously wondered too many times if we should have just let him go be with God but I usually kept it to myself, because hope was all any of us had, at that point. I kept the kids away for the first month, because it was devastating for me to see dad like that, with tubes here, there, and everywhere. I did not want the kids to see him like that, if I could possibly spare them of that, and I knew that dad would not want them to see him that way either.

He was on a respirator, had a feeding tube in his stomach, and could not walk, talk, swallow or do much of anything at all. Many times, I would fight back tears as I looked at him, wondering what we had done to this man, who had been so virile and independent. Meantime, my mother pushed and yelled at him to do things that he just couldn't do. Dad also had suffered from renal failure, and had to have kidney dialysis three times a week. Those sessions exhausted him and left him totally drained. He seemed to just exist.

By mid May, there was talk of moving him to a different facility, as he could only stay in the ICU for so long. Whenever I tried to talk to the caseworkers about possible places to move dad so that he could see his family regularly, my mother would go ballistic. She would tell me that since I was not paying the bills, it was none of my business. Between my mother and the caseworker, they made plans against everyone's wishes to move dad to a hospital in Chicago that could accommodate all his special needs. My mother always made her position clear; she was in charge, she was his wife, and they would do, in the end, whatever she wanted. She was able to get a ride out there twice a week to see him, and didn't care if any one else got out there to see dad. Voicing all my concerns, I asked her a couple different times if we couldn't just drive out there to check this place out first ourselves, but she insisted that this place was fine and that we had no choice where dad went, anyways.

She was also getting tired of the sympathy and concern that we all had for dad. She hated seeing his brother come up there, and became so irate with him, that the poor man left, infuriated. My mother had gotten in his face, over a comment my uncle made, at a time when the poor man probably did not know at all what to say to his brother, but wanted to say something cheery. He said to dad," Just lay there and relax and let the pretty nurses take care of you; that's what they get paid for." My mother went ballistic, telling him that the nurses wanted him to start using his arm on his bad side. The stroke had hit his entire left side, but ironically, did not seem to hit his face. She also told him that she hoped he himself would have a stroke, so he could see what it was like.

Of course, dad was usually conscious when these types of exchanges took place. I often wondered for a long time, what all must have gone through his mind.

Chapter 13: A Diary of Pain: The Spirit is Broken

May 17, 2000

Went up to see Dad today; mom was doing her volunteer work for Meals on Wheels, so it gave dad and I a chance finally, for some privacy, without her telling me constantly what to say and do.

He has a sadness about him that pierces my very soul, and haunts me at night. When I close my eyes to sleep, it's HIS eyes I see, in all their utter pain, sadness, fatigue, and futility. I asked him if he knew what happened to him, and why he was in the hospital, and he shook his head no. I asked him then, if he would like me to tell him, and he nodded yes. I told him about the massive stroke he'd had, and about the 9 hour surgery that he had endured, and a look of understanding passed through his eyes, almost like he was thinking, oh, no. He has a trachea tube in this throat and a feeding tube in his stomach, not to mention the oxygen tube in his nose. He tries to pull his various assortments of tubes out, whenever he is awake. His arm is unbelievably frail and thin. In short, looking at him now is breaking my heart.

I sat down and held his hand, and told him that I had some important things I needed to say. I needed him to listen, and asked him if he understood, and he nodded his head yes. I proceeded to tell him what an impact he has made on my life, how I have raised my kids the way he helped raise me, and that he has always been my angel on earth. I told him that when he went to be with God that he would still be my angel. Tears were streaming down my face while I was telling him all these things, but he needed to hear all of it, and I did not know when or if I would have the chance to be alone with him to tell him all these things again. Then I told him that if he ever decided that this was all too much for him, that it was okay for him to go be with God and just let go, and that I loved him so much that I do not want him to suffer. I also told him that this was a time for him to think of himself and not worry about what anyone else thinks or wants. I asked him if he understood all of this, and he nodded his head yes, and squeezed my hand hard. A few minutes later, I asked him if he was at all angry with any of the things that I had just told him, and he shook his head no, and squeezed my hand again. Later, I talked to him about our fishing days together and all the fun we had then, and have had throughout the years. There are times when he looks off to the side, with a vacant look on his face, and you wonder what he is thinking about, or what he is feeling.

He keeps trying desperately to tell me something, but can only mouth words, and not well enough that you can read his lips. I leave a few minutes after my mom gets there. She says that maybe she did wrong by letting him have the surgery, and that maybe we should have just let him go then. I tell her that we would have always wondered, in the back of our minds what would have been and that can be hard to live with. At least we tried, I tell her. I get out to the parking lot, and head back home. I barely get on the toll road, when my dad's face and eyes flash in my mind, and hot tears of pain and helplessness stream down my face. I want so badly to help him; this man that has always been so strong and healthy, now reduced to sitting in a chair with his head lolled to one side, looking so sad and defeated. I wonder what is in store for him, and if he will ever be better.

May 21, 2000

After many tears last night, over both dad's condition, and my dog's inability to stand at all from her hip pain, we all head out to the hospital. Before I had left Wed., my mom asked Dad if he would like to see my kids the next time I came up, and he closed his eyes tightly, as if trying to fight

43

off the tears, and nodded his head twice. It was very heart wrenching, but I guess everything is for me these days. I rarely get through a day anymore without crying, it seems. At first, Dad seems to not want to look at the kids, as if it is too painful for him to have them see him this way. I tell John and the kids to go downstairs and join my mom for lunch, so that I could sit down with him alone for a few minutes. I asked him how he's doing, and there are tears in his eyes again, when he finally looks at me. He is desperately trying to tell me something. I wish I knew what it was. After he finishes mouthing something to me, he slowly turns his head to look me square in the face, staring at me, as though waiting for my response. My heart is breaking for him, but I just squeeze his hand and tell him that it's okay. He seems to be mulling all of this over in his mind.

I sat there and just talked to him, thanking him for all the unconditional love that he has always given me, and always loving me and being proud of me. It seems so important that I tell him all of these things, and I tell him how much I love him, and how much he has always meant to me. I tell him about Foxxy, my dog's physical decline with her legs and hips, and a look of understanding and sorrow passes over his face. He seems to understand everything I am telling him, and squeezes my hand in understanding. I picked up the card he got from all his co-workers and read it to him, along with all the names and messages. They all love him and miss him, and have all been touched by him in their lives. He is always so willing to help someone, and has a very accepting nature about him that lets people be who they are without judgement and ridicule.

Soon everyone is coming back in his room now, and my mom demands that I come down and eat lunch, as though there is even a remote chance that I could waste away. We leave John and the kids with dad, and I tell the kids not to be afraid; just talk to Grandpa the way you always do. Hold his hand and tell him what is going on in your life. I tell dad later that his granddaughter scored her first goal in soccer today, for him, and that seemed to make him happy.

I feel sad and empty, when it is time to go. I feel like I never want to leave his side, but I know that I must. He finally waves goodbye to all of us, and I tell him that I will be back again soon to see him.

I kiss him on the forehead one last time the way I always do, and tell him that I love him, and to try to hang in there.

I almost feel numb on the drive home, but apparently not numb enough, because I start to cry once again.

That night, I try to pray, and ask God to touch him and make him better, or to take him to heaven, if this is all he will ever be now. That is all I was able to pray, because the pain is too intense.

May 24, 2000

After an early morning hair appointment, I got on the road to go see dad. The trip seemed endless, stuck behind a semi that never went faster than 50mph. In truth, I just couldn't seem to get there fast enough. When I arrive at the hospital, dad is in intensive care still. He is sitting up in a chair, but his head is leaning off to the side, to the point that he looks like he will fall off at any time. He does not want to be moved, so I fight off the impulse to try to straighten him out in the chair, anyways. I kiss him, and tell him that I am glad to see him. He looks very sad today, and I ask him if he is feeling sad, and he nods his head yes. He looks straight at me for a short while, and then suddenly, starts mouthing to me almost furiously, and once again, I wish so much that I knew what he is trying so hard to tell me. I nod my head in understanding, and take his hand into mine. He squeezes it tightly, and I see the tears begin to well up in his eyes. Never had I ever seen my dad cry before this devastating stroke, but now the realization of what has happened to him, I am sure, makes him utterly depressed.

My sister Chris comes in, and together, we try to straighten dad out a bit. He just sits there and lets us move him. She tries to lighten the moment with a joke, but dad does not smile or respond; he just looks at her, almost as if to say," that wasn't funny." Chris looks at him, and says," don't you think I am funny," and dad just looks at her and shakes his head no. That was funny.

The nurse came in to give him his breathing treatment. She got everything set up for him, blew kisses at him, and got him to pucker his

45

lips back at her. That was funny too, and Chris and I were laughing. Chris was teasing him about having a girlfriend, saying, "What's your wife going to say about that," but dad did not respond to that.

My mom comes in, and Chris tells her about dad puckering up for the nurse, so immediately, my mom, the egomaniac, goes up to him and demands a kiss, and dad shakes his head no, and Chris and I start laughing. My mom must have asked him 4 times, well, demanded, I should say, before he finally kissed her and stopped shaking his head no. I kiss him goodbye, tell him I will see him again soon, and to hang in there.

May 27, 2000

Got up early today, because my mom says that they are moving dad to Chicago this afternoon. He was on dialysis when I got up there, and was very weak and exhausted, like he always is when he has had it. My mom says that now they are not moving him up there today after all and maybe not until Tuesday or Wednesday now. It is all a bit frustrating, as they are still not feeding him the soft foods yet. They say that they are waiting for him to be moved up to Chicago, and then they will insert a different trachea tube. The whole situation is very depressing. He knows I am here, but does not care much because he is so exhausted from the dialysis.

May 29, 2000

Today is Memorial Day, and all four of us go up to see dad today, in case they move him to Chicago tomorrow. My mom is waiting for her neighbor to come up, so that she can buy her lunch for taking care of her dog all the time. Of course, the minute we got there, she wanted me to go down and have lunch with her. Does she not understand that I do not drive all the way out here just to have lunch in the hospital cafeteria with her?

Already she is whining about how sick and tired she is of everyone feeling sorry for dad. Her point is that he is being taken care of, but who is taking care of her? Always, always, about her. As usual, she tries to control every situation, and starts bugging me again to come down with her now, but I would not back down. I sent everyone else down there with her and sat down next to dad. Taking his hand, I told him that I would keep him company, and asked him if that was okay. He nodded yes, and squeezed my hand hard.

After telling him about my week, and what is going on in my life, I bring up the subject of Chicago. I wanted to know if he knew and understood that he was going to be moved soon, and he sadly nodded his head yes. I told him that I would come up to see him as often as I could, but would not get up there as often as I could now. He squeezed my hand, and then squeezed his eyes shut hard. When he finally opened them, he had tears in his eyes. I could not help but cry some; it is so sad to know that he will not have the support of his family coming to see him everyday. I feel that is the one thing that has kept him going, and now I worry that his depression will only deepen. I know that he does not want to go to Chicago, but none of that really matters to my mom. No one, once again, has asked me for my opinion, and I can't help feeling frustrated and sad. I tell dad that even though I can't be with him as often, that I am always with him in thought and prayers and in my heart. With tears coursing down his cheeks, he slowly nods his head. Sometimes I wish so badly that I could help make some decisions, but my mom has already informed me, once again, that I am not paying the bills, and that he is HER husband, and that it is none of my business.

Tuesday, May 30, 2000

Today I find out through my sister, that now they are not sure if they are moving dad to Chicago or not. More frustration and agitation, as everyone plays the waiting game. After talking to my sister, she gives me the name of the caseworker at the hospital, so I call her. We have a lengthy conversation about my dad's condition and case, and we talk about my mother, who is starting to grate on many nerves over there. I ask her to keep our conversation confidential, and gave her the names and numbers of some places out this way, where at least, I could keep a close eye on dad.

Apparently, this ticks my mom off to no end. The next day I call her up to check on her, and she wastes no time lighting into me, telling me that

I had no business going behind her back, talking to the caseworker, and when am I going to just keep my nose out of her business. She goes on a long tirade, telling me that she is real tired of people treating her like she is stupid, and I tell her that no one is thinking she is stupid; we just all want to help, and there is no harm with everyone putting their heads together to try to help find a wonderful place for dad. She tells me that this is HER husband and why can't I get that through my thick skull? She tells me that she will never come live with me, because I am, and always have been, stupid, and she will not go live with someone as stupid as I am. She claims that she only listens to what the doctors say, yet, when they try to talk to her and tell her about dad's condition, she never shuts up long enough to hear anything they are trying to tell her, and ends up telling THEM what's going on with dad.

There has always been times throughout my life when I have just wanted to shake the shit out of her, but right now, it seems even more tempting. I tell her that I am sick of her insults, and if that is all she has to say to me, I am hanging up. I also told her that any other parent would be happy that their child was taking some initiative and trying to help. I made many calls that she would never make, because they are long distance, and she always claims she can't afford it.

She never even took a trip out to Chicago to check out this place, even though I offered to take her up there first, to see how we liked it. She claims that we don't have a choice where dad goes. I think to myself that she is full of it. The bottom line is, she wants him at this place because she can ride a van twice a week to go out there and see him, and the hell with everyone else. She could care less if anyone else in the family ever got up there to see him. She is the only person he really loves anyways, she would say.

Saturday, June 3, 2000

After getting up early, I drive out to my sister's, and then we go pick up my mom at her house, and head out to Chicago to go see dad in his new surroundings. As usual, my mom was her usual argumentative self; God forbid if someone has a different opinion than hers, because then they must be stupid. I want so badly to see him much more often than I am able to, but work and family commitments make the 5 and a half hour trip impossible to make more than once a week.

We find the place fine, but from the moment I laid eyes on him, the tears welled up in my eyes. He looks so pathetic, with his head laying off to one side and a vacant look in his eyes. He slowly turns to look at me, and the sorrow in his eyes made the tears run down my face. As if this in itself were not bad enough, he is laying in his own human filth. His left leg is so thin, as it dangles out over the side of the bed. The poor thing looks like a poster child, wasting away from starvation, and we find out that they STILL don't have him eating food yet, as they haven't inserted the different trachea tube. Swiping my eyes, I immediately leave to find a nurse who will clean him up. I am SO not impressed with this place already. A half hour later, someone finally comes in to clean him up, and we all step out into the hallway.

I had found a cute stuffed bear here in town that had a bigger bear with a smaller bear on its back, as though getting a piggyback ride. I give it to dad, and he seems to know me right away. I tell him when I give it to him, that I got it for him because it reminded me of the two of us when I was little. He seems to understand. He clutches the bear with his good hand in a death grip, not about to let it go.

He seems so depressed and very tired, and after a little while, it is obvious that he just wants to take a nap. Of course, all my mom can say is everyone came all this way to see him and it sure wasn't to watch him sleep. She keeps tapping him on the nose, trying to make him "do" things, that he obviously can't do, and trying to force him to stay awake. He gets angry, not that I blame him at all.

The woman is enough to drive any completely sane person nuts, and there are days when I honestly don't know how much more of her I can handle. She seems to thrive on keeping me, especially, as in the dark as possible, and I deeply resent that. I have hopes of bringing dad out here by me, where he would be much happier because he would have someone close by visiting him everyday. I want to spend so much more time with him, and monitor his condition closely.

Dad finally succumbs to his need for sleep, much to her dismay and disgust, and now is blissfully unaware of all her mindless comments.

We are all getting hungry, so after the second time that I suggested to just let him rest and leave him alone, we go across the street and have lunch. He is completely out now, and has the bear clutched tightly in his grasp. My mother tried taking it away from him, until she saw the look I gave her, and I asked her why she couldn't just let him be. We come back about an hour later, and the bear is still firm in his grasp. My mother seems angry that he likes that bear so much, probably because he loved something that I gave him. She has never been a compassionate soul, and is obviously not about to start now.

We are up there for two more hours, and then head back home. Dad can speak just a bit. He says hello a few times, and after my mother hounded him to death to say I love you, mumbled something to her.

I hated like hell leaving him there. The place does not give me a warm feeling at all. Maybe a part of it is that I have to get over wanting him close by me so badly.

Dad had hung onto my hand when we were ready to leave, and was not going to let go at all. I had to slowly pry my fingers off of his, talking to him the whole time, and telling him that I would be back real soon. Of course, my mom starts complaining again, and keeps saying that we have to go, telling me to "get away from him, so I can get over there," and on and on. She just never quits. God, I hate leaving him there all alone. I wonder if he feels deserted.

Sunday, June 15, 2000

Today is Father's Day. After spending the night in Portage at a motel, we all head out to the hospital to see dad. I had ordered a balloon bouquet for dad, from all three of us kids. Anything to brighten up his room a bit, I thought to myself. It was the most dreary and depressing place.

He seems surprised to see us, and I tell him Happy Father's Day, and kiss him. I ask him if he knows who I am, and he tells me right away, and takes my hand in his, and appears to be intently studying my face. John and the kids leave after a few minutes, to go have lunch and hang out, giving Dad and I some privacy.

In general, Dad's health seems fine, but I always wonder how his mind is doing. The speech therapist comes in, and I get a chance to meet her. She asks dad to identify different objects in the room, and asks him who I am. The only thing that confuses him is his age, and mine. I feed him his lunch when it comes up; it's so good to see him finally able to actually eat, even though the food is made very thick. The visit was great, and I actually left there feeling more hopeful than I had for awhile. Little did I know, that that hope would soon be slipping away.

Sunday, July 2, 2000

We went up to see dad again today. He is coughing and seems congested, but when I tell the nurses about it, they shrug it off, saying that he gets focused on one thing, and that he is "panicking about not being able to breathe." Excuse me? I really did not like that explanation much, because to me, it was not panic. With my experiences with panic attacks, I would like to think I know the difference between panic and congestion. I definitely could hear congestion, but finally I let it go, because I am not a nurse and figured they knew what they were talking about. At least, I would like to think so. He is not wanting to eat a lot for lunch, but he does eat some. He tells me that he just wants to get out of there, and I tell him that I will help make that happen anyway I can. He always says, "Help me" which irritates my mother to no end.

Sunday, July 9, 2000

Today, Dad has on an oxygen mask. He pulled out his trachea tube three days ago, and the hole apparently closes up right away. Unfortunately, he

51

can no longer eat, so now he is back with the feeding tube in his stomach. The nurse is full of reassurances, saying that all of this is temporary. I teased Dad about his fingernails being longer than mine, and he disgustedly looks at them and agrees. Whenever he wants me to do something for him, he always says, "help me," and then tells me what he wants me to do. I asked him if he would like me to trim his fingernails if I can find a pair of clippers and he says yes, that would be great. I get dad all clipped up, and he asked me if I could do his toenails too, so I did. They needed it.

Dad talks to me a lot today. He keeps telling me that he wants to go home, so after a few times of him telling me that, I asked him why he wants to go home so bad, and he tells me that he misses his kids. It occurs to me, that his mind is back about 50 years, and thinking that Jim and Chris are small again.

I told dad that he MUST stop pulling his tubes out, as it just makes his stay longer there in Chicago, making it harder for us to get him out of there. I explain to him why he has the feeding tube in his stomach again, and why he cannot eat, and tell him that he could choke to death or get pneumonia if anyone tried to feed him solid foods right now. He informs me that he would rather have pneumonia than choke to death, and I tell him that I would rather he had neither, thank you. He says okay, and asks me to wipe his eyes again. The steam that is coming out of the mask seems to irritate his eyes. He holds my hand and tells me he loves me, many times today. His eyes lock into mine, so many times, as though he is looking at me for the last time.

I also tell him that I am working on trying to get him into a different place in Indiana, and why he can't come home right now. I ask him if he would like it if I could get him into a better place much closer to me, and he quickly assures me that that would be wonderful. He asks me if I can make that happen. I tell him I am doing everything I can.

I was so glad to see him today, and I leave feeling confident that he will be okay, and get better in a few days. Little did I know that that confidence would soon be slipping away.

Friday July 14, 2000

How can someone look so much worse five days later? I asked myself that a few times all day today.

My brother and I went up to see dad today, because I had just found out that dad was in intensive care, battling pneumonia. Apparently, it only took them three weeks or so to figure THAT out. It was such a traumatic experience, seeing dad like that. He looks awful.

For one thing, he has not been dialyzed for a few days now, so his face, arms, and hands are unbelievably swollen. He is also on a ventilator now, which my brother says hurts like hell. He has that in his mouth, plus a mouthpiece in on the other side of his mouth so that he cannot bite down on the tubes, which would set off the alarm, from what his nurse told us. The whole scene is as gut wrenching as it gets, because on top of all of this, dad has tape running all the way across, from his mouth, to just below his ears, so that there is no way that he can take it off. They have also managed to tie his hands and arms down.

Obviously, there is no way that he can talk, and I can tell that he desperately wants to. There are tears in his eyes, and a look of sorrow and desperation on his face. It is a haunting look, silently pleading for someone to help him. The nurse tells us that dad needs dialysis, which we have already figured out. A part of me wants to just say, "No kidding."

Dad hasn't had a haircut for well over a month now, giving him a wild and wooly look, which would be bugging him to no end. He hangs onto our hands so tightly, and can do nothing but look at us, with tear-filled eyes. He has the look of a wounded animal that is pleading for mercy.

He begins to look as though he can barely keep his eyes open, so I ask him if he would like us to leave so that he can get some sleep, and he nods his head yes. I gave him his bear and he clings to it tightly, and a few moments later, he is asleep. Jim and I look at each other, unable for the moment to even speak, so lost in our own thoughts and sorrow for what is happening to dad.

We talk a lot on the drive back to his house, and we both wish that God would just take him, instead of him having to go through more and more suffering. I am angry anyways, because dad has a living will, which seems to come as a total shock to everyone up at this hospital whenever I mention it. My mother allowed them to put that ventilator down him, and I feel like that is so wrong. He never wanted to just keep hanging on like this, and it seems he knows that he will never get better. Sometimes I am starting to think that he wants to just die in peace. Jim and I talk about how unfair all of this is, and we hate to see him suffering so much, but all we can do is pray and wait.

July 17, 2000

Today was another emotionally, gut-wrenching day. I drove out to my sister's house this morning, where my brother was already waiting for us, and the three of us drove over to Uncle Will's to pick him up and take him up to see dad, too. Jim and I had spent time trying to prepare them for what they would see up there. Obviously, from the pain on their faces, and their confessions later, they never fully understood how bad it was until they got up there and saw him.

We are all dealing with so many emotions. None of us had ever approved of him being up there, but we knew we'd have to accept it, and we tried to. Yet it is so amazing to see how fast a person can deteriorate, and in such a short time. I have never believed that he got very good care up there, and of course my mom couldn't even be bothered to call up there to check on him. I have called over there so many times to check on his condition, and everyone up there gives me a different answer. Finding someone that speaks clear, good English has been an ongoing battle also, and very frustrating.

At one point, my mother had mentioned to Dad's doctor that he had been taking high blood pressure medicine before the stroke, and in fact, for the past 20 years. Of course, the doctor explained that it would be most helpful if they knew exactly what he had been taking before the stroke, and the dosage, as well. They asked on a Wednesday when she went up there, if she could call them when she got home and read the information to them. She told them, no, it was a toll call, and she would just bring the bottle with her when she came on Saturday, regardless of the fact that the doctor was not even going to be there on Saturday.

That was always one of the first things that she would bring up, is how "it's a toll-call for me, so I can't call." It used to make my sister and I so mad, that she would carry on and act like she was so destitute and could not afford it, when we knew darn well that she could. I just always felt like, despite her constant yelling at me about how this was HER husband, and she would make all the decisions, that she really didn't care that much.

By this time, she was really starting to reek from self-pity. She could never see that she had been blessed with him for 43 years, or anything else. When anyone, including and especially me would dare to feel pity and compassion for dad, it seemed to anger her, and she would say, "He's fine, he's being taken care of; what about me, though? Who is taking care of me?"

It has always been about her. Everything that happens to anyone seems to always come back to revolve around her. A truer egomaniac never lived. It pained us all to see dad so obviously suffering and in so much pain. He would just lay there in fetal position, with the tape and the ventilator and everything else hooked up to him. I wonder how much more the poor thing can possibly take.

Saturday, July 22, 2000

Today is dad's 82nd birthday. The four of us "bite the bullet" and pick up my mom and take her out to the hospital with us to see dad. For the most part in the van, she tried to maintain, but she can only do that for so long, it seems. She acted friendly enough on the drive out and back, and actually didn't boss me around as much as she usually does. I was impressed.

Dad seemed a bit confused today. I asked if he was on tranquilizers or something, but was told no. He almost acts like he is out of it a bit. Thank God he is back in a room again, and off of the ventilator. He still has the oxygen tube in his nose, though.

At first, he does not seem to know who I am, and he seems so troubled by it, which I can understand, but I assure him that it is okay. At one point, my mother went down the hall to the restroom, and I leaned over and kissed dad on the forehead. I told him I love him, and he started to cry. I asked him then what was wrong, and what was he thinking about that made him so sad, and he said, "You." I started to ask him why, but then my mom walked in, and proceeded to dominate the conversation, as usual. I told my mom what dad had said, and she just laughed, saying," you made your dad cry; that's terrible."

Dad unfortunately committed the ultimate sin, by calling my mom by his first wife's name.

That really ticked my mother off, to put it mildly. As I watched in total shock, she slapped him, which made me want to choke her.

I cannot imagine doing that to someone who is in the kind of condition that dad is in, and to someone that you supposedly love so much. I am hoping to get back up here later this week again, if I can. We sang happy birthday to him, and he seemed to understand that. Poor thing; to be in the shape he is in, on your birthday, stuck in that hospital. In the back of my mind, I wondered if this would be his last one.

July 27, 2000

My sister, brother, uncle and I all went up to see dad today. For my uncle, it was a great relief for him to see his brother off that ventilator. Dad seemed very aware of his surroundings, and was very talkative and insightful today.

He needed no prompting whatsoever today, when it came to who everyone was.

My sister and I took turns feeding dad his lunch. He is still on a special diet, of course, and everything has to be quite thickened, or else he would choke on it. He still has the feeding tube in his stomach also, from 7pm to 7am for added nourishment.

Dad was so thirsty today. He sucked down his milk and juice, and told me that it felt like there was something still stuck in his throat. I laughed at Chris, my sister, because she made him eat some of his vegetables, even though he did not like them at all, and did not want them. I told her that I don't make him eat that stuff he does not like, and she asked me if I do that with my kids, and I said yes.

I told dad I would find more milk for him, and Uncle Will followed me out. We managed to track someone down that was kind enough to get more of Dad's milk, so we went back to his room with it.

Upon our return, the room seemed strangely quiet. Chris and Jim seemed strained, but no one really said anything. Jim was staring out the window, seemingly lost in his own thoughts.

Strange, I thought, but immediately opened the milk up for dad, and sat next to him so that I could hold the carton for him as he drank.

If I had been curious as to what was going on while I was gone, I was not to have to wait too long to find out. Dad's mind seemed even clearer than usual today; certainly clearer than the last time I had seen him, when he seemed a bit confused about who I was.

Dad seemed to need to say some things, so he called Chris over to his bedside, and she took his hand. He told her that he wanted her to take care of things, and to clean everything up. She laughed at one point, and asked dad if he wanted her to go home and clean her house. Dad shook his head, and told her no; he wanted her to get everything organized, and get everything ready.

I was starting to find this conversation eerie, just because in my paranoia, I wondered if Dad was trying to tell everyone goodbye. I had heard often that people's minds are so clear right before they die.

Then he called Jim over to his bedside, and took his hand. He said," Jim, I want you to just do it; I don't care how you do it; just do it. Jim looked devastated, of course, and told Dad that he just could not do that.

After these two revelations, I considered the fact that there would not be much left for me to do, as all of the big, important tasks have been taken care of. Not to be left out though, I went and sat next to dad, and lightly asked him, "What about me, Dad? Do you have anything you would like for me to do for you?"

Dad took my hand and squeezed it tight. He said, "Yes, just one thing," and I said, "Okay, dad, you name it."

I will never forget it as long as I live, when he told me to "just do what you do best." I repeated it back to him, and he nodded and said it again.

I was not sure of what exactly that meant, but compared to my sister and brother, I felt blessed to have gotten off so easy. I also felt touched by his words.

This day was rough. On the one hand, I desperately want his pain and suffering to be over, and it is becoming painfully obvious that the only way that will ever happen now, is if he goes to be with God. The selfish part of me just wanted desperately for him to go back to the person he always was all my life, before the horrible stroke.

As time went on, it was becoming clear that that was not going to happen. Yet, I look at him, and feel my heart about to break, because I am not ready to let him go; I never would be. Life without Dad's voice, his touch, and looking upon that sweet face that I have always loved seemed unthinkable.

I keep praying and asking God to do what is best for Dad. I know that he knows what that is, because I sure don't anymore. I know with all my heart, that the last thing Dad ever wanted was to end up like this, which, of course, is the last thing anyone would want. As much as I love him and can't imagine my life without him, I just can't stand it anymore, watching someone I have always loved so much go through all of this.

On a day like today, I feel like the dull, constant ache that I have in the pit of my stomach will never go away.

August 8, 2000

Chris, her oldest daughter, and I went up to Chicago today to see Dad. Nothing ever seems to change with him. I feel so sorry for him; sometimes as bad as I miss him and want to see him, I almost dread going to see him, because I don't like what I see.

He never gets any better. His poor legs ache, his bottom aches, and he wants out of there so badly.

He asks me again today to PLEASE do whatever it takes to get him out of there, and I tell him that I will. In fact, I have already started working on it.

After feeding him some of his lunch, we talked with him for a while, and I was stroking his hair and forehead before I left. He was looking at me very intently, as though he was thinking about something. I asked him what he was thinking about, and he said, "You."

I said, "Me? What are you thinking about, when you think of me?" He said that he was thinking about how good I am. Sometimes I don't FEEL very good, knowing that he is up there by himself. I just desperately want to get him out of there, and somewhere close to me, where he can have a chance at getting better care and help, but once again, my mother controls the entire situation.

It is all so sad, and I feel so depressed when I go home. It is so hard to look into his eyes anymore, and not feel like a knife is ripping my heart open.

August 9, 2000

I am on a mission. I have spent much time this morning, talking to the caseworker, Colleen, about dad. I wanted her to know the entire situation, and she agreed with me that dad seems very depressed. I told her that I feel like he has given up, and that he says that he wants to die. She promises me that she will speak with the doctors and see what she can do.

August 19, 2000

We go up to see dad again, and I spent time with him, feeding him, and rubbing his legs down with a cream that I bought. It is supposed to be very relaxing and therapeutic, so I figured if nothing else, it would feel good, anyways. He has a couple toes wrapped up, and tells me that he broke them, but he does not know how. I am alarmed by this, and make a mental note to check into this. After lunch, dad holds my hand tightly, and I rub his forehead and hair gently like I always do after he eats lunch. It seems to relax him, and puts him to sleep eventually.

He looks at me with tears in his eyes, and tells me that sometimes he just wants to die. I tell him that I know and understand, but that I am working hard on getting him out of there, and starting to make things happen. With any luck I tell him, by September he will get out of there. He seems to cheer up at that, and I promise him that I will keep working at getting him out of there.

He asks me if I can take him home with me, and I tell him, I can't do that, but I wish I could. Dad then asks me if I brought my van today. I smiled and told him yes, and ask him why he asked. He was so cute, then, because as he continued to hold my hand tightly, he asked if I could just put him in the back of the van and take him back to my house with me. The moment was bittersweet, and I could feel tears welling up in my eyes, because I know how desperately he wants out of that place.

At least it seems like me talking a lot to the caseworker is helping, as she has been looking into all the possibilities of where dad can go. I told dad gently that I would love nothing

more than to take him home with me and take care of him myself. I know I would probably do a better job, too, as far as paying attention to him went anyways, but I don't kid myself for a moment that it would be an easy task. I explained to him that I just don't have the training or the kind of facility that he needs right now for him to come live with me, but that by getting him out of that hospital and into more of the rehabilitation setting that he needed, that the day would come when I could bring him home with me. We dreamed out loud together of the spacious bedroom that dad would have, all to himself, with a nice, big television to watch the Chicago Cubs on. It seemed to be a very soothing thought for him, because, for the first time, I saw him smile.

Labor Day Weekend:

Wanted so much to go see dad this weekend, but could not make it out there. The good news is that the place I really wanted Dad to be at in South Bend is probably going to take him, so he should be out there later this week. Haven't seen him for a while, but I will just wait now until he goes to South Bend.

Helped mom gather dad's things in a suitcase, and went with her to get dad some sweat pants and shirts so that he will be warm enough when he goes to South Bend.

Sept. 10, 2000

Dad had a brief episode with his heart going a bit crazy, so they have moved him to the special care unit. I found out by accident, calling up there to check on dad, and instead of connecting me to the floor that he is usually on, they connected me to Special Care. I immediately said that there must be some mistake, and told the person who answered the phone that I was looking for my dad and gave him his name. He told me that Dad was in Special Care, and proceeded to tell me why. He also told me that my mother had been notified the night before, a little before midnight, and that she had called over there in the morning to see how he was doing. Of course, my mother had not bothered to call me and tell me what was going on. No one else in the family knew either.

Sept. 12, 2000

Thankfully, dad is out of Special Care and back into his own room again, but his transfer has already been postponed twice, because of one thing or another. The doctors check him out and say that he is fine, and then the next morning, when he is supposed to be leaving, they say he has a fever, even if it is only 99 degrees, and won't let him go. We are all so discouraged by now, and wonder if Dad will ever get out of that place.

Sept. 15, 2000

The place in South Bend can't take Dad now. They waited as long as they could, and gave his bed to someone else that needed it, and I can't blame them for that. Now they are talking about having him moved to a nursing home not far from where my mom lives.

This whole thing is so depressing, although I am SO ready for dad to get back into Indiana, and out of that hospital. To add to the already impossible equation, now they are saying that he has a staph infection.

Dad finally gets moved to the nursing home. On Sept. 30, I leave early on Saturday morning, and drive to my mom's, and then we head over to the nursing home. Dad does not seem to be doing too badly, but I guess he has a hole in his back from the staph infection, and the bad news is that they say he has gotten another staph infection now, as well. I guess he has one last souvenir from that hospital in Chicago. Some days, it just feels like that poor man just can't win. It is always one thing after another.

October 4, 2000

I had such an awful night tonight. I just could not stop crying, once I had started, it seemed. Around midnight, I got out of bed, and came downstairs and turned the computer on. Suddenly, words jumped on the screen, and within 10 minutes or so, I had a poem written that I was happy with. And then the strangest thought occurred to me; I was going to read it at dad's funeral. Don't ask me why; maybe the whole idea of that poem and that feeling I had was to help me deal with the inevitable.

October 5, 2000

Dad has been in the hospital again, one last time. The decision was made by my mom, after talking to dad's kidney doctor, that dad would be taken off of dialysis. She had decided that it was time to stop everything that was just keeping him alive, and let him go. The kidney doctor told my mom that dad was soon going to be a vegetable, because he was never going to get better now. Another staph infection had started, not to mention the past month of him being quarantined because he'd already had one.

I never looked at it, but my mom and my sister told me that there was a large hole in dad's back. I decided to take their word for it, because I just did not want to see that, too. By this point, I was beginning to feel like I had seen enough; seen all that I could possibly want to see in a lifetime, watching all that dad had gone through for over 5 months. My mom called me and told me about her conversation with the kidney doctor.

I had fought the urge many times in the past, especially when he'd gotten the pneumonia, to tell my mom that I did not understand why dad had even bothered to sit down and write out a living will when obviously no one was going to even abide by it. I guess a living will gets real technical, though, because life-saving techniques seem to mean different things to different people, obviously. I had long since felt like dad had gone through more than enough, and as time was going by, and as painful as it was, he just did not seem to ever get better. I decided to take the next day off work and go in and see dad, since they were giving him 2-4 more days to live.

October 6, 2000

After the kids left for school, I got in the van and drove out to the nursing home, where dad would spend the last days of his life. My sister was planning to spend the day out there also.

My mother seemed almost cold and oblivious to the fact that dad was dying. As someone had put it to me, after she had made the decision to stop the dialysis and all, she seemed very matter-of-fact about it all. And to top it all off, my mother seemed to only be concerned about getting my sister and I to be witnesses to HER living will statement, and she spent several minutes tying us up with that, getting signatures and the proper notarization. A couple of times, I could only shake my head from total frustration.

And then, my mother chewed out the doctor that was assigned to my father, because he should have made sure that my mother was notified this last time, when they took my dad to the hospital, and all but called him a liar, despite all that he was trying to tell her. I certainly understood being upset about not being notified, and then coming in the next day, and not finding him there. That could be very upsetting, but all of this seemed to be a very moot point to me now, since dad was dying. My mother seemed oblivious to that fact though, almost as if she was on a different planet. Dad told me several times today that he loved me, almost as though he knew this was his last chance.

My parents' minister was a kindly man, and came in the afternoon to give us all communion with dad one last time. Dad really can't participate, since he cannot eat or drink, but his spirit is there and willing. After spending the whole day there, I head for home. I feel like everything is happening in slow motion, as though I am watching this happen to someone else, but I'm not. I spend the hour and half drive in a kind of autopilot silence. When I park my van, I don't even remember the drive. All I seem to feel now is a resigned sense of sorrow.

October 8, 2000

I left early this morning, and had an overnight bag packed that I kept in the van, as I had the feeling that dad would not last much longer. I don't know why I felt that way, but I just could not shake that feeling.

From the moment I walked into Dad's room, my mother seemed bound and determined to do battle with me. She snapped at me, almost immediately.

By now, everyone's astonishment at her attitude was quickly turning to disgust, as she shocked some family members the night before by discussing who would be dad's pallbearers, while sitting a foot away from him. Although on his deathbed, dad was still very coherent, and could obviously hear everything that was said. That just never seemed to stop my mom at all. I have always known that she was a very cold, selfish human being, but she seemed to be taking these traits to a whole new level.

Because of the staph infections, dad was still quarantined, and his room was at the very end of the hall, with explicit instructions on the door for all that entered that room. After donning the appropriate attire, I walked in and said hello to dad. He managed a "hi", and I took his hand, and kissed him on the forehead and told him I loved him, and he said," I love," which was all he could manage to get out. Because he no longer was being dialyzed, dad was drowning in his own sea of congestion and fluid, and the sounds he made when he had to cough gave me nightmares for a long time.

My mom started in on me immediately, and told me not to touch him, that he did not want to be touched today at all. So I came over to the chair next to her and sat down. After a couple of moments of discussing the snow I had driven through, she once again brought up dad's upcoming funeral, of course, with him laying right there.

At one point, I shook my head at her, and told her that this was not the time and place to be discussing this stuff, with him lying right there. Her response was, "Why? He knows he is going to die, so what's the difference?" I am sure that the horror I was feeling was all over my face, because I have never been able to hide those kinds of feelings well, and at this point, I wasn't about to try. To say that I was horrified by her attitude and comments would be the understatement of the year. For Dad's sake, I tried to just let it go.

The next comment immediately after, was for her to tell me that she wanted my son, who was 10 years old, to be a pallbearer, and to tell me who all would be pallbearers. I told her that I was not sure that I would have the kids go to the actual funeral, as my husband and I had not really discussed it yet. I also said that I felt that a ten-year-old boy was too young, in my opinion, to be a pallbearer.

She totally unleashed on me then, and told me that if I did not bring my kids to his funeral and show some respect and honor, then she would hate me for the rest of my life. Eventually, she simmered down, and then went on to ask me when I was going to come over and get dad's stuff out of her house. I was beyond words, because I just couldn't believe that she insisted on discussing all of this, right in front of dad. He barely talked at all now, as he obviously needed all his energy and strength to just exist, but I knew that he was still very coherent.

I asked about the morphine dosage that they were giving him, and my mom told me that they were giving him some every so often, which didn't tell me anything. I went out later to have a cigarette, because I was already too emotionally drained to deal with my mom's idea of a conversation. As I stepped outside, my sister pulled up and got out of her car, and I told her to be careful, as my mom was in rare form today, and was constantly angry at everything where I was concerned.

I went back in a few minutes later, and hung out in the room with them. My brother-in-law was there too, by then, and it was a relief to have someone else there with us, so that I did not have to deal with my mom alone. However, she snapped at my sister a few times too, but like me, she did her best to just let it go.

A bit later, dad's brother and sister showed up, accompanied by their families, and this seemed to make my mom even angrier. Uncle Will could not seem to say anything at all, without my mom jumping all over his case, but he seemed to ignore it pretty well. My mother hated the fact that my dad's family came to see him; she did not think much of them at all, and in her mind, since they did not spend much time with him before, they didn't need to spend time with him now. But she was a person who would complain no matter what. If they hadn't showed up to see their dying brother, she would've complained about that, too. There was never a point of ever making her happy or satisfied, and I don't ever remember thinking that my mom was a happy person. Maybe that is why she always went out of her way to make other people so miserable. Misery loves company, or so they say.

A bit later, after dad's brother and sister left with their families, my mom and my sister and brother-in-law decided to go to the little ice cream shop inside of this nursing home and get some ice cream. My mother asked me to come along too, but I said no, and usual, she demanded to know why.

I told her that I was lactose intolerant, didn't have any of my pills with me, and did not want to get sick, so finally she let it go. I sat in the chair and pulled it up close to the bed, and for a few brief moments, I told dad that I loved him so much. I held his hand and told him that it was going to be time for him to go soon, and that when he saw Jesus hold his arms out to him, he needed to grab those hands and just go with him. I felt strangely calm, yet unbelievably sad, all at the same time.

I had commented to my mom earlier, after Dad had had one of his coughing fits, that it sounded horrible, and I felt so bad for him. To that comment, my mother scoffed and told me that I "obviously have never heard the death rattle before and should not plan to be around when he dies because I just couldn't take it." As usual, she had to be ugly. It's true that I had never heard anything like that before, but it was a horrible, rattling sound that I would love to never hear again for as long as I live. She went on to make fun of me some more, and I just let that go too.

Right before my mom came back from her ice cream trip, a nurse came in to check on dad, and I asked her if she knew how often they were giving him the morphine, and she said that she would find out and let me know. I was curious as to how they would even know if he was in pain or not, because he wasn't really talking anymore by then, and he had been in so much pain for 6 months, that I did not want him to die that way, too. Moments later, the nurse came back and told me that they gave him a certain dosage every four to six hours, but that they had to be careful, because if they gave him too much, it would kill him. I thanked her, and thought to myself how utterly stupid that really was, since everything had been stopped so that he could die anyways. My mom came back in time to meet up with the nurse in the hallway, and she must have mentioned that I was curious about the dosage of morphine, because my mother came in and started yelling at me immediately, telling me that SHE had already told me about it, and when would I just mind my own damned business. I told her that I just wanted to know that dad was not in anymore pain than he had to be in.

She would have continued to rail at me in her usual relentless fashion, but was interrupted by that same nurse, coming back in the room. The nurse gave my mother a stern look and reassured me on dad's dosage of morphine.

After she walked out of the room, my mother picked right up where she left off for another minute or two, and then told me that I was sitting in HER chair, and would I please move, so I did. My mother seemed so far gone in her mad rages that day, and feeling the need to lash out, especially and constantly at me, that she no longer seemed to care what anyone else thought of it, either. And she certainly had no problem yelling at me the whole time in front of dad, laying there on his deathbed. I remember feeling a wave of intense sorrow for him. I figured that if he had not had a whole lot of peace in his life with her, the least she could have done was let him die peacefully.

A few minutes later, dad had another bad coughing attack, and I got up and walked over to his bedside and gently stroked his forehead and whispered to him to try to relax; it was okay. I kissed him on the forehead and stroked his hand for a moment, and he squeezed my hand. I walked back over to my chair and sat down, and my mom lit into me again. "I told you when you got here, to just sit down in that chair and not move. He doesn't want to be touched, and he doesn't need you laying on his bed, bothering him."

I calmly told her that I was not lying on the bed at all. In fact, I didn't even touch it; I just leaned over it for a minute, and that was it. She was rapidly building herself up into yet another rage, and told me that she was sick and tired of everyone feeling so sorry for him. SHE was the one that was suffering and alone, and needing someone to take care of her, and then went on to tell me that he was fine, because he had people taking care of him.

I bit my tongue one last time, fighting off the impulse to say that apparently, he was not fine at all, or he would not be on his deathbed, for crying out loud. Then, she told me that no one has understood these last six months how hard all of this has been for her, and that everyone only thinks of themselves and their own grief, but not hers. She railed at me for the total lack of sympathy I, especially, showed her. I told her that that was not true; everyone has their own pain to deal with, and the relationships have all been different, but it does not make the pain any less. I understood, I told her, that this was her husband, and that we all wanted to help her, but that she needed to remember that everyone else was in pain, as well.

I also pointed out that this was my daddy lying, there, dying before my eyes. My friend, my buddy.

With a dark look, she scoffed at me, saying," Oh please, you have never loved him a day of your life. You only went to see him when he was in Chicago once or twice, and that was only out of a guilty conscience."

Rage like I had never felt before began coursing through my body, and I started shaking violently from head to toe. I couldn't even speak, because I no longer trusted anything that could come out of my mouth, at that point. I also couldn't be anywhere around her, because I was far too angry and hurt. With one last look at the first man I had ever loved, laying on his deathbed, a fresh wave of tears hit, and I stalked over to the hazardous bin by the door. In record time, I ripped the gloves off my hands, and started taking off the gown and hat. Without a moment of remorse or conscience, my mother proceeded to taunt me, by yelling," Stop acting like such an ass, and come over here and sit back down." I seemed to no longer hear whatever she continued to say after that, and with a final yank, I ripped the gown off and through it into the basket. As I pulled the door open, my brother-in-law was sticking his head in the doorway to say goodbye, and my sister was putting her proper attire on. The look on their faces was priceless, as I managed a goodbye. My sister walked in, and my brother-in-law hurried down the hallway to catch up with me. I shook like a leaf, and stayed and talked with him for a few minutes, telling him all of what had happened. After that, I climbed into my van, and headed home. To this day, I don't know why, but I know I wasn't thinking straight by then, either, because I had planned to be with dad when he died. I was adamant that I didn't want him to be all alone there.

I wasn't home 2 hours, and the phone rang, and the news was not good. They were calling everyone to tell them that dad was getting much worse, and that it would not be much longer now. As I hung up the phone, I sat down at the kitchen table and cried my heart out. I was so angry at myself for letting my mother chase me out of that room. It seemed like I just kept replaying the days' events in my mind, and I finally made myself quit, because I knew there was nothing I could do about it now, but the pain I was feeling had just intensified.

My first impulse was to jump in the van and head back out there, but it was an hour and a half drive, and I had already driven through a whiteout twice that day; once on the way out there, and then on the way back home. I also worried that I would not make it in time either, if I did go. After talking to my husband at great length, I decided to wait until the next morning, and then drive back out there again.

At 12:30am, the phone rang, and I leapt out of bed nervously and grabbed it, fearing the worst. My brother had just gotten home, and wanted to give me the latest report on dad. Surprisingly, dad had rallied in the late hours of the night, and finally, everyone left around midnight to go back home.

A half hour later, my sister called, with much of the same news. My mother had asked if I had been notified, surprisingly, but no one told her if I was coming back out, because no one knew for sure.

At 6:30 the next morning, the phone rang. It was my mother, calling to tell me that dad was gone. I remember feeling calm about it at the time, just because I was so relieved for him that it was finally over. The six months of pain and suffering was finally over for him.

My mother didn't talk long; she did not seem in the least bit interested at all in how I might be feeling, either. I asked her if she was okay, and she said yes, and hung up.

I took that day off of work, of course, and went through so many ranges of emotions. I made many phone calls, and looked at pictures of dad, and cried with such intensity, I thought my heart would break in two. The whole day seemed to be that way, an uneven balance, between relief for dad that he was now at peace, living the good life with God, and the intense pain of knowing that I would never see him here on earth again.

My mother was supposed to call me that afternoon and let me know the particulars, concerning the funeral and visitation, but, of course, I had to find out this pertinent information from other people, namely my sister. I had called my mom that afternoon to check on her, and apparently, she was doing just fine. Within an hour of going to the nursing home, where dad's lifeless body lay, she was out at a restaurant that she frequented, eating breakfast and socializing as though nothing was the least bit amiss.

I was finding her harder and harder to take, as it just didn't seem like she was very affected by dad's death at all. All she seemed remotely concerned with, was the fact that she had looked through dad's suits, to see which one she would bury him in, as she said, and told my sister, and then me, that she had found over $4000 in a suit pocket. Somehow that didn't surprise me, because I knew that my dad had kept a stash of cash somewhere, but I never knew where, and had never bothered to ask.

The spring before I got married, my parents had been getting ready to go on a trip to Hawaii, as they did most every spring, up until the last couple of years. Dad had followed me out to my car, with a mischievous grin, looking like he had a secret to share. He glanced furtively around for a moment, and then dug into his pocket of his trousers, and pulled out a $100 dollar bill and pressed it into my hand. I remember feeling a bit shocked and surprised, and although I was very touched by the gesture, I did not want him to give me his money that he had earned from his part-time job. I told him that, and shaking his head, with a glint in his eyes, he told me that there was a lot more where that came from, and told me to just have fun while they were gone.

Memories came flooding back to me, and the greatest pain for me of all, was not seeing dad one last time, and it pained me horribly to know that he was alone when he died. I had really wanted to be there with him when he died, and because of my mother's hatefulness, I left and went home, when I just knew, deep down, that it was almost over. It took a long time to get over that feeling of pain and sadness, but I finally came to the realization that perhaps it just wasn't meant to be. For the last week before he died, I had been telling a few people that if it was God's will, I would be with dad when he died. Maybe God knew that it wasn't the best thing for me.

October 11, 2000

Today is dad's visitation. Everyone kept saying how great he looked, but at some point, I just wanted to scream, after the 20th time I heard that. I thought, how great can he look; he's dead. But I guess compared to the gauntness of his face, and his coloring, while he had been so ill those six months, through makeup and all, they were able to make his face look fuller, like it had before.

I think that I must have been in shock that day, to a degree. I rarely cried, and whenever I took a friend up to look at dad, it seemed very unreal. The visitation went as well as could be expected, although everyone was on edge, wondering what exactly my mom would say and how she would act, especially where my brother was concerned. Whenever my friends came, and I took them up to see dad, my mother would shove us out of the way, because she had someone more important that needed to see him. She said that my friends didn't matter.

I was touched by all the people that dad had worked with that came to his visitation. Most of his co-workers were there, crying with sadness, many of them, teenagers. I would greet each person, introducing myself to them, and felt touched that each one told me what a wonderful, sweet man he was, and how much they would miss him.

The minister knew that I had a poem that I had written that I wanted to read, and after reading it, he encouraged me to read it during the short service after visitation was over.

At 9pm, the viewing was officially over, and the minister wanted to have a short service. He also told us that we would all look at dad one last time tonight, and then when everyone left, the casket would be closed for good, as they would not re-open it tomorrow. My mom, my family, and I went up to look at dad last, and when my brother had gone up there with his sister and wife, he was crying and my mother was mumbling hateful things under her breath, and to me. I told her to just let it alone; this wasn't the time or the place. She shut up then, but I could tell that she really hadn't wanted to.

When the minister had finished, he announced to everyone that I had written a special poem that I would be reading, and invited me to come up front and read it. Here's the poem that I wrote a week before:

He was the one that made me feel so safe and secure.
And gave me the strength I needed to endure.

He was the one that taught me what unconditional love meant,
And I carried it with me wherever I went.

He was strong, yet gentle, and we'd sit contentedly,
And when I would talk, he would listen to me.

And whatever I said, he treated it importantly,
It mattered to him, if it mattered to me.

I could spend hours, and sometimes we would,
If the water was calm, and the fishing was good.
He was my buddy, you see, and he loved me just for me.

He never cared much about whether I would make a lot of money,
Or if I had an important job; he just wanted my days to be sunny.

My happiness was a joy, and my sorrow, his pain.
And if I hurt him or made him mad, He never did complain.

We had a lot of laughs, daddy,
Some great times together too.
But now you're gone and my heart aches,
Because I'm missing you.

I know the fight you fought, laying week after week in that bed.
At least you're safe and happy now, and in heaven instead.

I never wanted you to suffer, not after all you've meant to me.
But I wasn't ready to let you go, nor would I ever be.

You will never know how badly, I am missing you now, dad.
But I am just so thankful for the memories I have.

I never could say goodbye; parting brings such sorrow.
You are a part of my heart, now breaking, and it will still ache tomorrow.
But you have always looked out for me, and somehow I just know.

That you are now a special angel in heaven,
Watching out for me here below.

I know you're hanging out with God, resting your eyes, and relaxing somewhere.
But don't forget our fishing gear; we'll need it when I get there.

Most people had tears in their eyes when I finished, and busied themselves blowing their noses, and swiping at their eyes. I am shocked that I made it all the way through reading that poem, without totally losing it and breaking down.

My mother, seemingly the only person in the room looking unaffected, seemed to not even notice. She never said a word about the poem, that night, or anytime after.

October 12, 2000

Today was the day that I really had dreaded. I, like most people, I'm sure, have always hated funerals. I think that we hate the finality of the whole business, because, like it or not, that is the day when the pretense ends. That is the time that the reality of the situation starts to really hit. I think to a degree, I was still in shock.

I had thought for sure that I would fall apart horribly at the funeral. The actual funeral was at my parents' church, and the only time things started to go haywire, was right before the funeral got started at church. Apparently, my mother the control freak, thought she would dictate who would sit where, and starting ticking people off, with her ideas. Chris was sitting in our pew with her husband, but then my mom told MY husband to sit in the pew behind me, which did not go over well at all. I could see a flash of anger in his eyes, but he started to get up and do as my mother told him. My sister decided that this was utter crap, and told John to sit back down, next to me, where he belonged. Then my brother wanted his wife to sit next to him in our pew, and my mother told her she couldn't sit there, and my sister-in-law got up, and started walking away, until my sister stopped her. I could see trouble brewing, and my first thought was please, not today of all days. Thankfully, it all got resolved quickly, and the service got underway.

My mother rode with us to the cemetery, as she decided she did not want to ride in the hearse with dad, to his final resting place. I thought that a bit strange too, but did not give it much more thought.

After the service at the cemetery was over, we all rode back to the church for the luncheon, and my mother heckled my nephew numerous times about coming over to her house immediately afterwards, to get a gun of my dad's that she had found.

My Uncle Will tried his best to be kind upon leaving after lunch, and told my mother to take care of herself. Her reply was, "What the hell do you care?"

It seemed beyond her to treat anyone well at all, except for the two friends she still had. She seemed to move heaven and earth to make sure that they had food and were comfortable but seemingly, everyone else could just go straight to hell, for all she cared.

We left a few minutes after lunch was over, to head home. Our dog had been at the kennel, and we explained that we needed to go get her before they closed for the day.

The drive back home seemed surreal, as had the past 36 hours. A part of my brain just could not accept this at all, but then the part of the brain that knew better would step in, and the tears would flow. I never knew a person could cry as much as I did these past six months; sometimes, I thought that at some point there wouldn't be any tears left to cry. But, when I least expected it sometimes, there they were.

How was I going to live the rest of my life without him, I would ask myself. It seemed to be expecting too much, most days. In addition, while I was very thankful that I had my children and my husband, and good friends in my life, a piece of my heart would forever be missing. In addition, a chapter, a very long chapter of my life, was ending. For saying goodbye to daddy was like saying goodbye to all the good and wonderful things of my childhood. It meant really having to let him go, and the thought of never seeing him again until I myself went to be with the Lord felt so unbearable.

Chapter 14: Life without Daddy

October 20, 2000

Today I drove out to what was now, just my mom's house. That in itself seemed a bit too weird, and a part of me hated going in there and having to face the fact that Dad would never be there again. But as usual, my mother was oblivious to anyone's pain and grief but her own. Although she seemed not to really be suffering much at all.

She was determined to get all of dad's stuff out of the house, the sooner the better. That alone was difficult for me to fathom, but the real pain for me, was going through all of his clothes and belongings. It was a few hours before we were finished.

My mother hovered around, mostly to ensure that I did not come upon any extra cash that dad might have stashed away. And I didn't, of course. Eight huge garbage bags later, all of his suits, clothes, ties, shoes, and etc. were packed away, the closets looking bare and empty.

The bear that I had brought to dad on my first trip to see him in Chicago sat on the dresser, and, like a respectful dummy, I asked my mom if I could have it, and she of course, said no, could she just keep it for awhile, and I reluctantly said okay. I hauled the bags out to the van, and it was very full by the time that I headed for home. My living room was filled with bags for a few days, as I wasn't about to just "throw it all out", or "give it all to Goodwill", as my mother had advised.

November 4, 2000

We all drove out to my mom's today, because she insisted that we help her "clean out the garage." That in itself was a joke, because dad was one of the neatest men I had ever known in my life. Things were neatly stored in the garage on shelves, and she had plenty of room for her car in there. Once again, my mother was determined to get rid of anything that had been his.

I insisted on bringing the kids today, too, if we were coming at all, I told her. And she was in such a big hurry to get that garage cleaned out, that she reluctantly agreed, but told me that "her nerves just couldn't hardly stand anything so she hoped that they would be quiet and stay out of the way."

This was her usual answer, and she had not seen the kids since dad died, but she did not want to see them, either.

I had tried to help her out, in any way I could. Each time I came out, I asked her about Thanksgiving, and what her plans were. Her answer, once again, was "Oh, how should I know; that's too far away?" Thanksgiving was now only three weeks away, and I got tired of asking. To me, it was simple. Yes, you would like to get together, or no, you do not.

I was also getting ready for my hysterectomy, which was another reason I just wanted to get out there and get that garage cleaned out, because cold weather would be setting in soon, and I did not want to hear about that damned garage a thousand times, as if anything in there would grow wings and fly away.

When we were leaving, I happened to mention to my mom that it almost seemed like dad had never even lived there now. Her comment to me was that she did not need any of his stuff, so why would she keep it? I just shrugged my shoulders and let it go.

I asked her about dad's beautiful onyx ring, and I should have suspected that she just flat-out lied to me, the way that she acted. She told me that it had just disappeared, and that she didn't know where it was, and hadn't seen it. A couple weeks later, I found out accidentally through my sister, that my mom had given it to my nephew when he had come over to take the gun, and since he didn't want it, he'd given it to my brother. I was glad that my brother had it; it just blew me away that my mom would lie about it, instead of just telling me the truth. Then again, it sure wasn't the first time she had ever lied about something, that's for sure.

November 10, 2000

Early this morning, John dropped me off at the hospital to check in for my hysterectomy, and went back home to get the kids off to school. The surgery had been scheduled for around 9:45, but they wanted me there at 8am. I had told John that there would be plenty of time for him to get the kids off to school and then come back out to the hospital before they would be taking me away for surgery. I was wrong. The plans had changed, and five minutes after I was shown to my pre-admission room, a nurse bustled in and told me that they needed to get started on me, as my doctor was waiting for me.

For some reason totally unknown to me, I was apprehensive about this surgery. Not really scared, just more apprehensive than anything else. Of course, John's biggest fear of not getting back in time to see me before my surgery looked like it was about to come true. I felt very alone and scared, not to mention it was a whole month after dad had died, and the wounds were still too fresh.

About that time, my pastor walked in, sat down on the stool next to my cot, and asked me how I was doing. As he waited for my reply, the tears started coursing down my face, faster and faster. I told him that I was so sorry; I did not really know why I was crying, and asked him to forgive me for becoming unglued.

He took my hand, and told me not to worry about it; that tears were actually a gift from God. God's gift of helping us get through our pain and grief. He seemed to understand that so much had been happening in my life; just losing dad and going through those months of his illness, and now this hysterectomy, which, he added, can be tough on women sometimes, as it is so final.

I also told him that I was afraid that I would not see my husband before I got wheeled away to surgery, and he promised that he would stick around and wait for him, and make sure that he found where I was. Everything was happening faster and earlier than the original plans.

True to his word, he made sure that John found exactly where I was supposed to be, so that I was able to see him before my surgery.

The surgery was very uneventful, which was a blessing. Part of my fear, was also because I had had a laparascopy, hysteroscopy, etc., earlier in the year in March, and the paralytic agent kicked in on me before I fell asleep. That was one of the most terrifying few seconds of my life. My whole body was paralyzed, but my mind was still awake.

Unfortunately, I could not breathe, and was desperately trying to tell them that, but could not speak either. Mercifully, a few seconds after that, I went to sleep. I have since made sure to warn friends and acquaintances, not to scare them, but in the hopes that this sort of thing won't happen to them if the need for surgery arises. I have heard of this a few times, since I had my experience.

Thankfully, the anesthesiologist assigned to me for this surgery, was a sweet young woman, who seemed to think that there was no way that this should have ever happened to me before, and assured me that it certainly would not be happening today. I felt assured by her strength, and started to relax.

November 11, 2000

I got to go home today. Having a vaginal hysterectomy was so much easier than having the old abdominal surgery. Having had two c-sections, it was nice to not have to go through the abdominal healing like that again.

It felt good to go back home, although everyone at the hospital treated me wonderfully.

My mother called that evening to check on me, and once a couple days later. I was down and feeling blue that day, and as usual, she had to start on me. I mentioned that I was already getting bored with having to just sit around and do nothing, especially the first few days. The worst thing about that surgery was getting my strength back. As usual, all that my mom could do was talk about herself, and the surgeries she had had. She has always had everything worse than anyone and everyone else.

I started writing this book a week after my surgery. It had been ever present on my mind, and having a couple weeks off from work to just kick back at home and relax was just the excuse I needed. I figured, if nothing else, it would be good therapy for me.

A week before Thanksgiving, I called my mom to check on her once again, and she was hostile. She had just had cataract surgery on her other eye, and was yelling at me because "she had no one to do anything for her".

"I have to do everything myself," she yelled, as though I could help her if I wanted to.

I reminded her that I had just had surgery, and her reply was sarcastic. "Yes, I know, but you still have people doing things for you." She whined and yelled about the fact that I was of no use to her. I did not come out often enough and did not do enough for her. That seemed to be a big part of what I always went through with her, throughout my whole married life. It was always, and would always be, about her no matter what.

On Thanksgiving Day, I made the mistake of calling my mom to wish her a Happy Thanksgiving Day. To say that she was rude and hostile was quite an understatement. She told me that she hoped that I was quite happy with myself, and what a miserable excuse I was for a daughter, making her have to spend the holiday all alone. I reminded her that we had asked and invited several times, but that she would not commit to anything, much less even give anyone a straight yes or no answer. Of course, she denied that we had ever even invited her, and asked me when I had done so. I told her that the last time we had been in, we both had asked her about Thanksgiving and that she had told us that she just couldn't think about that right now.

"Well, what do you expect; I was busy cleaning out the garage, and couldn't be bothered answering your questions," was her answer. She then went on to let me know once again, what a miserable excuse I was, how I just came in to "put on an act for the world," (whoever THAT is), and droned on for a couple of minutes, unleashing her fury on me, via the telephone, until, quite suddenly, she hung up on me.

She had treated me badly the last few times I had been on the phone with her, and my husband warned me that maybe I should re-think that idea of calling her on Thanksgiving Day, but I did anyways.

That attack on me was to be the final straw for me. I had always put up with her verbal attacks, because I needed Dad in my life, and I would have done anything to keep the peace back then, if for no one's sake, but mine and his also. But then, I would have done anything for him, period. Now, however, it seemed to be a whole new ball game.

Since dad died, I have often wondered if you see things down here on earth as they really are. Maybe you didn't want to see it while you are alive. But I truly believe that you DO see it when you are living with God. How can you not? Everything is so perfect up there, while things down here are, well, you get the picture.

Five days before Christmas, I decided to call my mother and leave the toll-free number where we could be reached while we were in Florida. She always lets the answering machine pick up the message first, then gets on the phone herself, if she wants to talk to the caller. I started to leave my message, when lo and behold, she gets on the phone and starts to cuss me out. Big surprise. NOT.

"Why the hell would I want that damned phone number?" she yelled into the phone, as though I were deaf. "I just thought it best if you had it, just in case," I replied, wishing to God that I hadn't even bothered.

First, I got the usual story about how I could just leave her, newly widowed at Christmastime, to go off with my husband and kids. Never mind that this vacation had been planned for over a year, and that the kids were really looking forward to going to Disney World. She had told me a couple times before, that they could just wait. It would not kill them to wait another year or two, according to her, because, as usual, her needs and what she wanted should be the only thing that really mattered. She then told me that her needs were much more important than theirs right now, and if I were any kind of a daughter at all, I would put her needs first, ahead of theirs or my husbands'.

She also chose to bring up the letter I had written her, about a week after Thanksgiving. I had decided that enough was enough, where her abuse was concerned. I did not see at all why I should have to continue to put up with it, so I gently but firmly told her in this letter that we would like to have her in our lives, but that I was no longer going to put up with her abusive comments. I also told her that if I did not hear from her at all, then I would know that she didn't really care about me at all, and did not wish to be a part of my life any longer.

She angrily told me that she still had that "damned letter," and that since those were my words, then I should be able to figure it all out. I was quickly figuring a LOT of things out, it seemed. She was telling me goodbye, and seemed perfectly okay with that. I knew that it was a gamble when I wrote and sent out that letter, however loving the letter was. I just knew my mother. I had mentioned in that letter that her treatment of me, the last day I saw dad alive, and the horrible things that she said were false, and unnecessarily mean. She replied that I had it all coming to me, and should have had even more coming to me, because that is what I deserved, since I never, ever bothered to go to Chicago to see my dad. Of course, she'd had no idea at all how many times I'd been up to see dad, because I never told her. She didn't want to be around my brother at all, and seemed to think she could just pick and choose who she could get rides from.

She knew of that past Father's Day, when John, the kids, and I went up to Chicago to see dad and take his balloons up there. She'd gone ballistic upon finding out that we'd gone out there and hadn't asked her if she wanted to go. How could I even fathom going up there without taking her along?" she railed. "Just who the hell do you think you are, that you can drive out there and not take me," she yelled. She also asked me where I had gotten off, knowing that she would have liked to have gone, and reminded me that she only got to see him twice a week. I told her that that was at least one time more than I ever saw him. Most of the time, I didn't fight with her too much, but I did tell her that it was my vehicle. She told ME that under no circumstances was I to "pull a move like that" ever again. As usual, it was all about her and what she wanted. I just let her rant and rave, which seemed to be how I spent most of my adult relationship with her.

She brought up all of this too, and proceeded to cuss me out on the phone, calling me names. Quite abruptly, she hung up on me, and the first thought I had was, "you just made a big mistake, mom." Because for me, it was really over now.

March, 2001

The winter was passing rather uneventfully, which was good, but I was still having bad days, where dad was concerned.

It seemed like I could go a few days and feel fine, and then collapse into a mound of tears. By now, my husband figured that I should be starting to get over this. However, I felt like he just didn't understand.

He suggested that perhaps I go talk to someone. And, in some ways, it was almost better talking to a stranger that had to sit there and listen to you, ask you questions, and let you cry, talk, etc. It was also good to know that I was very normal, at a time when I was starting to wonder how normal I could possibly be.

The counselor was a neat guy, about mid to late 40's and very easy to talk to. The first time I went to see him, I had to fill out a checklist of things I had experienced in the last year to two years. Financial difficulties, illness of a loved one, death of a loved one, marital problems, and moving. In another words, check, check, check, check, and check.

I almost laughed at the look of utter surprise on his face to see all those things checked off. He told me later in that session that normally, most people will have checked off one or two of those but not most of them, and I made a joke of how I always have to be different.

We covered a lot in our sessions together. He concluded, by the end of my first session with him, that my mother was literally nuts. And he made sure that I understood that he was not kidding, or using the term loosely. I laughed, and told him to tell me something I didn't already know.

We did a lot of talking about my dad, and that last day that I saw him alive. I told him that everyone acts like I need to just get over it, and that I am dealing with it, and trying to live my life the best way I can. I emphasized that my father was a Christian, and that I knew where he was. I just missed him like crazy, and it seemed to be the worst thing of all for me, trying to get over that pain of not being able to see him anymore.

I had slowly but surely been working through the waves of grief when they would hit. A person learns a lot about themselves, too, after they have gone through something like this. Sometimes you don't even know exactly what triggered the pain, but in the end, it doesn't really matter.

After several sessions with my counselor, I was starting to put it all behind me, but even as I write this, I know it to be a ridiculous statement. A person can never put a loved one's death behind them, because it just does not work that way, anyways. Truth be told, we don't ever WANT to forget. Forgetting, it would seem, would be the ultimate death.

While I was beginning the long road back from the intense pain I had inside of me, the Lord blessed me with new friends and new opportunities.

Although I knew daddy was in heaven, I longed to know what his world was really like. I knew, without any doubt, that he was happier than he could have ever been in this life.

Meantime, though, I searched a lot in the bible, trying to find out what heaven was really like, and not finding the answers I was looking for. It made for interesting reading, without a doubt, but during my saddest hours of grieving, it still seemed that all I wanted was some kind of sign. Don't ask me what kind of sign; there was just something inside of me that, try though I might, hadn't let daddy entirely go yet.

April 15, 2001 Easter Sunday

Easter has always been a precious holiday to me. A different kind of magic than Christmas, but magical, nevertheless. And it would seem that that feeling only enhances as I get older. Maybe a lot of it now, is just knowing the sacrifices our Lord made for us. As a parent myself, I couldn't do it. The pure act of love, in the most unselfish form possible can't help but draw me to God, and to his precious son.

The agony, pain, and suffering. However, unbelievably, that has helped me, especially where daddy was concerned. Watching dad all those months, feeling so helpless, I know Jesus must have felt utterly helpless too, as his body screamed in nonstop pain on that cross.

The hatefulness I have experienced in my life is totally unmatched to the abuse that God's son had heaped upon him. Instead of asking why me, it quickly becomes why not me? For those who do not understand, it is not about what we do or don't deserve. If it were, we couldn't possibly imagine what lay in store for us.

This Easter Sunday seemed beautiful to me in a different way this year. I was accompanying the church choir on the piano, as well as various instrumental accompaniments to Handel's Messiah Hallelujah Chorus. I can't begin to explain how moved I felt while I was playing, listening to the sheer beauty of the music and words.

It was during the second service, about halfway through the song, when for the briefest moment, I had a vision. It was the strangest thing, but while I was playing, I looked upward towards the heavens, and could see a large group of people, singing, and grinning from ear to ear. It was like they were happily celebrating Christ's resurrection with us. And among those people was my father. He looked happy, relaxed, and very well. However, as suddenly as this vision appeared, it was gone. These people did not have wings, but somehow I believe them to be angels.

I savored that beautiful moment. It meant a lot to me, because it came from God. That night, I fell asleep and was not thinking of anything in particular. But I had the most awesome dream a person can ever be blessed with in their lifetime.

Resurrection is for real

There has never been any doubt in my mind that the resurrection is real, and yet, I think the concept is still hard to grasp, at least for most of us. I always had so many questions, and still do. Some say that I am the great American thinker. Always thinking, wondering.

The dream I had on Easter night was the most real I have ever had. I am convinced that it was God's way of bringing daddy to me, and giving me the comfort and peace that I had yet to find.

The dream starts out in a cemetery, where my dad is buried. I must warn you, that this will seem to be a most strange and bizarre dream in some ways.

I am there, for the first time, spade in hand, and ready to begin digging, so that I may finally plant the flowers that I have thought about planting all winter. And then it happens.

After the first thrust into the ground, the earth seems to move, just enough to make me wonder if it really happened, or if I just have an imagination working overtime today. After pausing for a moment, I decide that it is the latter, and thrust the spade into the ground once more.

Now the earth shakes even more, and suddenly, a hand appears out of the ground, and the fingers move up and down, as if to wave. I am not scared at all in this dream, which tells me it is a dream for sure, because I would have been running all the way back to my van, otherwise. I look at this hand, and wonder seizes my brain, because I would recognize that hand anywhere. That wide hand, and those shorter, stubbier fingers. That is daddy's hand, and it is waving at me.

I turn around to look behind me, but not a soul is there except me. I have work to do though, so I thrust the spade into the ground one last time. I am determined to plant these beautiful flowers for daddy. But as the spade hits the dirt one more time, the whole ground is now trembling violently, and suddenly, without any warning, dirt is flying everywhere. In my face and hair and anywhere else close by.

After I lift my face up, having picked most of the dirt out of my hair and cleaned off my face, I am shocked to see daddy, sitting up now in the ground where he was buried, an arm outstretched to me, as if wanting me to help him out of the hole.

I remember grabbing his hand, and then the dream shifts to the house I grew up in, in Gary. I was sitting in the kitchen, eating a bowl of cereal. My mother was never anywhere in this dream. I was about thirteen years old and looked as I did at that age, and my dad looked as he had, as well, back then. Suddenly, the door opened and daddy walked in, grinning his dimpled grin. I sat there, just staring at him, as he said hello.

Finally, he asked me what I was staring at, as he came over to ruffle my hair. I told him that I thought he had died. He then laughed his merry laugh, and told me not to be silly. "I would never leave you," he said. Then the alarm clock went off.

I will never forget that as long as I live. The first several moments I was awake, all I could do is cry in pain and agony. It felt like such a cruel joke. But as the day slowly wore on, I began thinking differently. I had been talking to a friend on the phone when it hit me.

"Oh my gosh," I said to her. "What is the one word that means Easter?" I asked her, knowing that she would answer my question correctly.

"Resurrection," she answered, not disappointing me at all. And then it really hit me. Here, the day before, we were celebrating with all of heaven, I'm sure, Christ's resurrection. His in-your-face to Satan, and death. Suddenly, I knew that finally I would really begin to heal.

June 9, 2001

This was a strange day. Maybe one of the strangest. The kids and I finally got our chance to head out to the cemetery. We were all excited to finally be able to plant those flowers that we had longed to plant, and to see the spot where Grandpa was buried. But nothing could have prepared us, especially me, for the shock of seeing that, not only did my dad not have any kind of marker at all, but to add insult to injury, my mother's stone was laying at the top of where daddy was buried. All kinds of things went through my mind, it seems, and whatever positive healing I had done, had temporarily just gone out the window.

We found out later, that the government was supplying my dad's footstone, as he had been in WWII. About a month later, he got a stone. Right name, right date of birth and date of death, wrong war. And even though I was not happy that they managed to screw that up, for me, at least there was something there for daddy. It broke my heart when there was no marker or anything there for him. It was as if he were a nameless, unmarked person.

At least now, when I go out there, until they fix the stone, and replace it with the right one, I can at least still plant flowers, and see daddy's name on the stone.

October 2001

It is almost the one year anniversary of daddy's death. In some ways, it is so mind-blowing to think that he has been gone for a year already. It just does not seem possible, and yet, what a year it has been. A year that has taught me about grief, love, friendships, family, and myself.

A year of getting closer to God, and perhaps coming a little bit closer to understanding some other things, as well.

I wish I could tell you that the pain is completely gone, but I can't, for to tell you that would be a lie. I am confident that there will always be some pain, for the simple fact that I will miss my daddy for the rest of my life.

For anyone that reads this story, that is hurting and grieving, my heart goes out to you. I know how you feel. I hope that you are getting the love and support that you need. That can be half the battle. You can do it alone, but you shouldn't have to.

For one thing, faith that the Lord will not abandon you in your times of grief will get you through. I have also learned that the people that are the least understanding and sympathetic are those who have never gone through the process of losing someone that they desperately loved. They have advice for you, but they are unqualified to give it. They have not lived through the experience themselves, therefore, they have a hard time emphasizing with anyone going through the pain of their loss.

I have also learned, that through no fault of their own, people will go out of their way to NOT talk about your loss. They think they are doing you a favor, but they are not. Your pain and heartache is real, and the loss of that person you so desperately loved and will always love, needs to be validated. In addition, those memories live on inside you, and they can't stay a big part of who you are by closing the book forever and trying to forget. A forgotten person has truly died.

Grief knows no timetable. What one person grieves over for a month, is another person's heartbreak for months. As long as you understand what you are feeling and going through, that's all the matters, without feeling the need to always explain your feelings. Realize that it's not important that everyone understands, because some may never understand. That is okay.

This past year has also been a time of coming full circle, as I call it. I have had to deal with the pain and suffering of an abusive parent, and a childhood that was not so perfect. I still deal with the pain of that last day I saw my father alive, and the fact that I wanted to be

there with him when he died and was not. I sometimes wondered why God had taken the parent that I loved so much as well.

Years ago, I would often wonder why God had allowed me to be put in that situation. If God loves children so, why does he allow them to suffer?

Now, strangely enough, I don't lament that childhood. It was far from perfect in some ways, and certainly, where my mother, her rages, and the abuse were concerned, nothing I would want any child to have to go through.

On the other hand, what an opportunity lost had it have been so. Life with different parents would have meant a childhood without daddy. A life without him. Without knowing that good, loving, sweet man. A man that lived and gave unselfishly. A man that thrived on being a daddy, not just a father. The man with the big dimpled grin, who touched lives and hearts, just by being himself.

Just do what you do best, daddy had said. Even as his world had crumbled, as life as he had always known it came to an abrupt halt, and he was left to deal with a body that was ravaged and worn out, he was encouraging me and loving me unconditionally, as he always had. Telling me that just being me and doing those things that I do best was plenty good enough.

I realize now, that by being blessed with daddy all these years that I have always had a bit of heaven. For when you look into the face of one who loves you unconditionally, you have the most beautiful view of Christ.

Epilogue:

Today is the one-year anniversary of daddy's death. It almost seems unreal, in some ways, that he has been gone this long, yet I have had a few moments today of reliving the sorrow of losing and missing him.

I had thought that maybe I should call my mom today and see how she was doing on this sad, one-year anniversary. My intentions were good, but the outcome was not.

She did not intend to carry out a calm, loving conversation with me. Within moments of calling her, I was under an attack that didn't end until I hung up on her, unable to take another moment of cruelty and pain.

Apparently, she was determined to sink as low as she possibly could. She knew that there were very few things that she could say that hurt me much anymore, but today, she sunk to a new, all-time low. She began by telling me that my dad had never wanted me, had never wanted to adopt me or anyone else, for that matter. She had to "talk him into it," she explained. She felt that she should also let me know that he was forever disappointed in me, and wished that they'd never adopted me. The more

93

she "talked", the louder she got, until she was screaming at me, asking me what it was that I wanted from her.

"All I ever have wanted from you was your love," I said. "Love has to be earned and deserved; it isn't freely given," she said, crying and screaming into the phone all at the same time. "I have never loved you, and will never love you, because you have never done anything in your miserable life to deserve it," she finished. "Goodbye," I said, feeling orphaned and alone, on the one day I didn't want to be alone.

My husband, especially, couldn't believe that I had bothered to even call my mother, and asked me what I had been thinking. I guess I had just wanted to be compassionate, and wanted to believe that eventually everything would be okay and work out. Now I knew that that wasn't what she wanted.

I had tried, off and on, for a long time, to extend the olive branch, show love and kindness, at least so that she could watch her grandchildren grow up, and be a part of their lives.

The last time I talked to her on the phone, she again called me names, and then accused me of turning my children against her. I told her that she managed to do that just fine all by herself, and that I'd had to do absolutely nothing to help that along. Meantime, my son had picked up an extension, and was listening to her cuss me and yell at me, in her usual fashion.

I guess at some point, and that moment was finally it, a person just realizes that some things in this life aren't meant to be. It has always struck me as sad, that my mother has always believed that everyone else is stupid and sick, and that THEY have a problem, but she doesn't. You can't help someone get well, and you can't force them to get help, if they adamantly refuse to believe that they have a problem.

She lives her life alone, not seeing her grandchildren grow up or much of anyone else, but I have concluded that she has chosen this life for herself.

I decided to take my pastor's advice and honor her from a distance. A card, a small gift for a birthday or a holiday.

I never believed anything that she told me that day. I have always known and believed in my dad's love for me. He loved me then, and he loves me now. His love was always one thing I could believe in and count on. I still can.

Letter From Heaven

Dearest one, whom I adore,
I never could have loved you more.
You gave such love while I was living,
Your love for me so freely given.

I tried to stay, but I could not.
The fight, now over; the battle, now fought.
It was time for me to go,
But there are things you need to know.

I felt the peace, then I saw his face,
Together we traveled through time and space.
And then I saw him shed a tear,
For those I leave behind, so dear.

The warmth of your smile, like a sunny day,
Would lift my soul, when life seemed grey.
Your tender heart, the cheek you would kiss,
All of these I will surely miss.

Your love made my life here so complete,
Your love for me, a gift so sweet.

Forever I hold you in my heart,
Just as I have, right from the start.

We will always be together, you and I,
As sure as there is wind and sky.
Rejoice with me, in times of grief,
That from this world, I have found relief.

I'll never shed those tears of pain,
My heart will never break again.
And when your earthly journey is through,
I'll be right here, waiting for you.

About the Author

A native of Indiana "Loving Daddy" is Niki Jordan's first book. In 1999 she completed a course through the Institute of Children's Literature and has plans to write for children and teens. A poet as well, Niki enjoys writing poems that speak from the heart.

An animal lover, Niki's family includes 2 dogs and 2 hamsters, a loving husband and 2 fantastic children. They share life together in northeastern Indiana.

Printed in the United States
23021LVS00006B/355-363